MAHABHARATA

MAHABHARATA

THE EPIC AND THE NATION

G. N. DEVY

ALEPH

ALEPH

ALEPH BOOK COMPANY
An independent publishing firm
promoted by *Rupa Publications India*

First published in India in 2022
by Aleph Book Company
7/16 Ansari Road, Daryaganj
New Delhi 110 002

ISBN: 978-93-90652-90-7

1 3 5 7 9 10 8 6 4 2

CONTENTS

v

PREFACE

I do not recall when I first heard the name *Mahabharata* and when I started recognizing the stories from the epic as being from it. It happened without my being conscious that the epic had started surrounding the space for the mythic construction of the cosmos for myself. Throughout the years of my growing up, literary works, plays, films, oral narratives, calendars, paintings, and motifs drawn in the public space in my village kept bringing to me various episodes of the *Mahabharata* story. A lot of the language that was spoken around me and the language that I spoke, without my knowing, reinforced the deep connection between the epic and me. Later, I went to colleges and universities to study literature. There, an unwritten convention about what could be, and what could not be, studied as literature signalled to me that the *Mahabharata* was not to be, or could not be, part of that study. As a teacher of literature, though I did some experimentation with how and which literature was to be taught, I remained well within the invisible unwritten conventions and biases of 'discipline'. Then, I decided to shift track, to go out and work with members of the Adivasi community. There, I heard live performances of a different *Mahabharata*. That ignited my desire to revisit the epic. Life, by then, had become crowded for me. There were always the unfinished assignments, pending deadlines, and compulsions of what I must write. Besides, there were demands on my time and mind arising out of my activism. During the rare moments when I was on my own, I used to promise myself that someday I would revisit the *Mahabharata* and see for myself what it means, at least what it means for me.

Then one time, when I was in the seventh decade of my life, a strange virus swooped down upon the humans. They decided to lock down life, with everybody asked to stay inside their dwellings. Universities, schools, offices, factories, farms, streets, wars, parties, theatres, and public halls, all were kept under lock and key. The sun and the moon became distant. Only TV and digital screens were kept alive for talking about the virus and spreading other viruses. Being on my own, I thought I would open the book of my memory and pen a portrait of a poem that has been speaking to the nation for two millennia. I have done it in the hope that the future world is free of all viruses, tangible and abstract. My mind is at peace with the future.

G. N. Devy
September 2020

1

THE EPIC QUEST

POSITIONING THE EPIC

It is hardly necessary to say that the *Mahabharata* is an extraordinary cultural production. It ranks among the very greatest in the entire range of world literature, and, within its genre, the epic ranks very high. It has exerted a profound influence on the thought and life of millions in the subcontinent, and it continues in our time to influence life in numerous ways. It would be no exaggeration to say that the *Mahabharata* has provided the horizons of imagination to Indian culture and civilization. Since it came into being, it has survived through recitals, renderings, revisions, translations, poetry, and fiction; through adaptations in theatre and dance and through representations in sculpture, painting, cinema, TV, and digital media. In India, kingdoms and dynasties have come and gone; religious sects have emerged, come to be popular, and declined; schools of philosophy have been formed and replaced by other schools; art forms have emerged and in subsequent eras been overshadowed by other art forms. However, the *Mahabharata* has never ceased to excite its audiences and viewers. It has not ceased to offer every individual, time and again, opportunities to connect with it. It has also allowed individuals to dig into it and disagree with it on many points. It has not been made dull by time.

If one were to think of it just as a story bringing together myth, legend, history, and pure imagination, the narrative is simple: a devastating war fought between cousins, with almost all the regional contemporary rulers of the time aligned on one or the other side. The story, read at this level, is spread over five generations, while the war itself is fought over eighteen days, each day bringing in new twists and turns into the narrative. The major characters are Shantanu, Ganga, and Satyavati of the first generation; Bhishma, Vyasa, Vichitravirya, Chitravirya, Chitrangada, Amba, Ambalika, and Ambika of the second generation; Pandu, Kunti, Madri, Dhritarashtra, Gandhari, Vidura, Krishna's father Vasudeva, and some acharyas, mainly, of the third generation; Karna, the three sons of Kunti—Yudhishthira, Arjuna, and Bhima, two sons of Madri—Nakul and Sahadeva, Duryodhana, Dushasana and their ninety-eight brothers, Krishna, Balarama, Shakuni, and an array of other kings and princes who join the action, in the fourth generation; and Abhimanyu, Uttara, Ghatotkacha, and many named but minor characters of the fifth generation. These are only the main characters.

There is also a much larger cast of characters in the form of servants, messengers, soothsayers, charioteers, fighters, and mythological persons, offering quite a copious representation of types—human, supernatural, and from the shadow world beyond reality.

Then, there are the numerous brothers of Duryodhana

and Dushasana named in the poem: Dussaha, Dussalan, Jalagandha, Sama, Saha, Vindha, Anuvindha, Durdharsha, Subaahu, Dushpradharsha, Durmarshana, Durmukha, Dushkarna, Vikarna, Sala, Sathwan, Sulochan, Chithra, Capachithra, Chithraaksha, Chaaruchithra, Saraasana, Durmada, Durvigaaha, Vivilsu, Vikatinanda, Oornanaabha, Sunaabha, Nanda, Upananda, Chithrabaana, Chithravarma, Suvarma, Durvimocha, Ayobaahu, Mahabaahu, Chithraamaga, Chitrakundala, Bheemavega, Bheemabela, Vaalaki, Belavardhana, Ugrayudha, Sushena, Kundhaadhara, Mahodara, Chithrayudha, Nishamgi, Paasi, Vrindaaraka, Dridavarma, Dridakshatra, Somakeerthi, Anthudara, Dridasandha, Jarasandha, Sathyasanda, Sadasuvaaka, Ugrasravas, Ugrasena, Senani, Dushparaja, Aparajita, Kundasai, Visalaksha, Duraadhara, Dridahasta, Suhastha, Vatavega, Suvarcha, Adityaketu, Bahawaasi, Nagadata, Ugrasaai, Kavachi, Kradhana, Kundhi, Bheemavikra, Danurdara, Veerabaahu, Alolupa, Abhaya, Dhridhakarmavu, Dhridharathaasraya, Anaadhrushya, Kundhabhedi, Viraavi, Chithrakundala, Pradhama, Amapramaadhi, Deerakharoma, Suveeryavaan, Dheerkhabaahu, Sujaatha, Kaanchanadhwaja, Kundhaasi, and Virajasa. Yuyutsu is Dhritarashtra's son by a Vaishya wife.

The events depicted in the *Mahabharata* vary from the thrilling, romantic, heroic, tragic, apocalyptic, and liberating to the mundane, esoteric, arcane, and enigmatic. The rush of the narrative takes one from event to event and sentiment to sentiment—at all times thrilling, mesmerizing, and captivating. The spread of the epic too is distinctly vast.

Among the ancient Indian literature, the Vedas were and continue to be restricted to a miniscule minority of specialized scholars. Other epics and sagas in Pali, Prakrit, Sanskrit, and Modern Indian Languages, barring the *Mahabharata* and *Ramayana*, are known mainly to advanced level students of literature and culture and exist only as names to general readers. The ancient plays are known only to audiences seriously interested in theatre. While their performances for a general audience were not uncommon in the first half of the twentieth century, there are not enough actors or directors who can present them with ease. There are various forms of theatre and dance and various levels of literary expression drawn upon ancient Indian texts that relate to specific social classes. But the *Mahabharata* and *Ramayana* continue to appeal to all classes, readers from many languages, and to persons of all ages as the timeless literary heritage of India.

What is it in the *Mahabharata* that gives it its timeless magic? Is it the mythical heroic characters with which the work is replete and their extraordinary lives that make the *Mahabharata* such an enchanting work? Or is it the epic tenor of every character's action, culminating in a great war, that explains its spellbinding charm? Is it the great wealth of profound philosophical and metaphysical thought present in it that dazzles the mind of its audience? Or is it the combination of all these in an unparalleled manner that makes it ever-fascinating to every audience, spectator, and reader? And, most of all, what is the reason for its unrivalled allure on the subconscious of millions of its audiences through vastly different cultural epochs? The sheer volume of commentaries on the *Mahabharata* that try to provide answers to these obvious questions is awe-inspiring. Among the great literary works in the world which have received unending critical attention are the Greek epics of Homer (*Odyssey* and *Iliad*), Dante's *Divine Comedy*, William Shakespeare's plays in the West, and the *Ramayana* in India. The *Mahabharata* has a justified claim to be on this list. This epic is, no doubt, a superlative classic. It is not my aim here to provide a volumetric measure to substantiate the claim but, without an iota of doubt, I would like to state what has been obvious to me over the last five decades of my study of literature. No other writer or literary work in the world has so far been able to surpass the *Mahabharata* in eliciting the number of responses, commentaries, interpretations, translations, and every manner of transformation and renewal of the original text for creating new works. I am not making this statement in order to establish that the *Mahabharata* is any 'greater' than any of the other classics mentioned above. Literary greatness is not a matter of any fixed 'values', such as the atomic number of a chemical or the speed of a bullet. Greatness of various classics at best admits individual appreciation. Never does it fit into a mechanical comparison with other great works. I mention the phenomenal attention received by the *Mahabharata* to point to a unique difficulty that one encounters while attempting to understand why it has survived for so long.

The earliest known version of the epic in the oral tradition was called *Bharata* or *Jaya-itihas*, a saga of a triumph that has at its heart the great destruction which one must accept on its own terms. Tradition, however, assigns the name Vyasa to the great poet who composed the epic. A closer scrutiny tends to reveal that the historic claim to its authorship has certain peculiar difficulties. The poetic energy, intellectual range, and philosophical depth of whoever created it are so stupendous that a comprehensive analysis of the *Mahabharata* becomes a challenging task. It leaves one so spellbound that it hardly becomes possible to state with any degree of certainty what it is all about. Is it only a string of stories, an unending and breathtaking torrent of episode after absorbing episode, with no purpose apart from depicting the life and times of the Kuru clan and its great war? One likes to ask: does it have a purpose in stringing the tales together? The standardized version of the epic has some 88,000 verses, distributed in ninety-seven cantos, placed in what the Western epics call 'books', or 'parvas' in the Sanskrit tradition. There are, in all, eighteen of them, in the sequence *Adi Parva, Sabha Parva, Aryana Parva, Virata Parva, Udyoga Parva, Bhishma Parva, Drona Parva, Karna Parva, Shalya Parva, Suaptika Parva, Stri Parva, Shanti Parva, Anushasana Parva, Ashvamedha Parva, Ashramvasika Parva, Mausala Parva, Mahaprasthanika Parva,* and *Svargarohana Parva.* Together, they cover a vast array of topics, amply justifying what Indians have believed in for centuries, that there is nothing in the cosmos that is not present in the *Mahabharata.* The question that comes to one's mind is, what does this vast mass of literary depiction intend to do? What indeed is its purpose? What do all these long books achieve as a single literary entity and as a single spectrum of imaginative depiction of things near and distant?

In order to grasp the full significance of these questions, it is necessary to refer to the distinction introduced by late eighteenth-century European scholars, in the context of their own epic tradition, between 'written' epics and 'oral' epics. Their conceptualization of the epic genre assumed that a written epic has a 'unity' in its structure. The ancient Greek philosopher Aristotle had argued while discussing Greek literature that tragedy has a 'unity' of place, time, and action. He proposed that tragedy needs to be played out within a 'single' place, 'single' time, and 'single and continuous action with a defined beginning, middle and end'.[1] Centuries later, after John Milton had produced a pair of epics, *Paradise Lost* and *Paradise Regained*, the eighteenth-century view expected a written epic, with its authorship known to the readers, to have a 'unity of purpose'.[2] This view held that as against the written epic, the oral epic normally is more of a rambling string of ballad-like compositions. An oral epic has, it was argued, a hero and other heroic characters, though the action in it may not be organized within a single space and the time depicted in it can be broken into irregular periods, long or short. The *Iliad* of Homer, classified as an oral epic, brings to life a relatively short span of time at the end of the Trojan war. The *Odyssey,* the second epic assigned to Homer, runs over a span of twelve years. In other words, literary critics three centuries ago felt that it was not necessary to ask an oral epic its purpose or theme. Its primary function is to

---

[1]Aristotle, *Poetics*, S. H. Butcher (trans.), London: Macmillan, 1902.
[2]Ibid.

reflect the norms and features of an ancient society and to tell a grand story. Beyond that, the oral epic has few other objectives. Of course, the assessment of epic literature in the West has undergone much change during the last three centuries. Particularly ever since the study of myth started gaining interest in the fields of anthropology and psychology, oral epics have received a more hospitable response from literary critics. It needs to be remembered that every epic is peculiar in the cultural and literary functions it draws up for itself. No two epics can be equated or compared without being unfair to one or to both of them.

Students, the reading public, and the audiences of folk performances until the early twentieth century had a relatively more direct access to Indian epics. Later, an increase in printed literature, cinema, radio, and TV brought in other modes of imaginative expression.[3] As a result, epics started occupying a reduced space in people's imagination. There was nothing particular in my schooling and upbringing that would have offered me any special avenues into understanding the epics as more than just interesting stories, but also as content consciously structured by a creative mind. I took to studying epics as a postgraduate student only because it was necessary to pass the MA examination. An assortment of epics was taught by teachers who did not have any great familiarity with them. Therefore, as a student, I used to subscribe to the

---

[3]*Ramayana*, the series, was the most successful television show aired in India in its time and left a huge impact on audiences. See Rahul Verma, 'The TV show that transformed Hinduism', *BBC*, 22 October 2019.

traditional European distinction between the oral epic and the written epic. It was convenient for literary classification. When documenting literature of the indigenous communities in India became my main intellectual preoccupation during the 1990s, I discovered that some epic traditions which could be described as 'oral' were still alive in the country, since they had not been not printed till that time. I also saw these epics appearing in print form within a few years of my exposure to them as living oral epics. Through multiple intimate exchanges with the singers of the epics, I realized that the superficial distinction between the oral and the written epic may not work well in the case of works like the *Ramayana* and *Mahabharata*.

It was then that my mind began urgently asking questions such as: What, if at all, is the central theme or purpose or the organizing principle that gives the *Mahabharata* its unique and unrivalled grandeur and magic? Why is it that no critic in India's long literary history has ever fully stated it? And, while the *Mahabharata* is so often described as India's national epic—or at least, one of its national epics—why has the caste-divided Indian society still not become a 'nation', a substantially homogenous people, despite its exposure to the epic for thousands of years? I grapple with these questions in the following sections, not so much in the hope of providing any fully convincing, definitive, and incontrovertible answers, but rather in order to formulate these questions with the critical gravity that the *Mahabharata* deserves. I would like to hope that, at some point in the future, the questions I am trying to formulate here may be revisited by some scholar or thinker who may be able to secure some answers. If and when that happens, these questions, and responses to them, could change the way we respond to the *Mahabharata*, indisputably one of India's greatest national epics.

REMEMBRANCE OF THINGS PAST

There is a considerable uncertainty about who wrote the *Mahabharata*. Was it Vyasa or another poet named Krishna of the Dark Island—Krishna Dwaipayana—or were these different names for the same person? If the hypothesis that there were two different poets is to be accepted, there is also a lack of clarity about who preceded whom. Was it Krishna of the Dark Island who produced the first, shorter version of 24,000 verses of a composition meant for purely oral purposes? And was Vyasa a latter-day scholar-poet who sat down and toiled for years to produce the compendious corpus of 100,000 verses that we know as the *Mahabharata* today? The text of the poem that we now have with us mentions a third 'writer' of the poem in the opening cantos of the epic. It narrates that when Vyasa wished to compose the epic, he wanted a scribe, and Ganesha was asked to fulfil the role. Ganesha accepted the responsibility on the condition that Vyasa would not stop at any time during the dictation. Vyasa, in turn, demanded that Ganesha would write down the verses only if he fully understood them. At one point during the process, Ganesha's stylus snapped. In order to avoid a pause, he quickly broke off one of his tusks and continued to write. Thus, in a purely technical sense, Ganesha is the 'writer' of the *Mahabharata*. However, this story does not appear in any of the manuscripts collected by the Bhandarkar Oriental Research Institute from South India. The 'authorized version' prepared by the institute places this story as a footnote and not as a part of the main text. Besides, it has to be kept in mind that the widespread reverence of Ganesha as a divine personage, as the son of Shiva and the brother of Kartikeya, began only after the texts collectively known as the Puranas started getting written after the third century.

The uncertainty about the exact author of the *Mahabharata* leads us to describe it as an oral epic as against the *Ramayana*, whose written composition preceded the first written rendering of the *Mahabharata*, and whose authorship is ascribed to Valmiki without any doubt. However, the distinction between an oral and a written epic, which is helpful for understanding the distinction between Homer's Greek epics and those by Dante in Italian and Milton in English, is not so entirely helpful in understanding the difference between the *Ramayana* and the *Mahabharata*. In this regard, one must bear in mind an insightful comment made by a twentieth-century commentator of the *Mahabharata*, Sri Aurobindo. He proposed, in a long essay comparing Valmiki and Vyasa[4], that while Valmiki was a greater poet capable of dwelling deep into the minds of his characters, the *Mahabharata* of Vyasa is a greater poem as it captures the political and philosophical significance of things that would have remained unobserved by a lesser poet.

---

[4]Sri Aurobindo, 'On Vyasa and Valmiki', *The Harmony of Virtue: Collected Works,* Vol. 5, Pondicherry: Sri Aurobindo Ashram, 1972.

'The poem was, therefore, first and foremost, like the *Iliad* and *Aeneid* and even more than the *Iliad* and *Aeneid*, national—a poem in which the religious, social, and personal temperament and ideals of the Aryan nation have found a high expression and where its institutions, actions, and heroes in its most critical period received the judgements and criticisms of one of its greatest minds. If this had not been the case, we would not have had the *Mahabharata* in its present form. Valmiki dealt with a great historical period in a more universal spirit and with finer richness of detail but he approached it in a poetic and dramatic manner; he created rather than criticized; while Vyasa in his manner was critic far more than creator. Hence, later poets found it easier and more congenial to introduce their criticisms of life and thought into the *Mahabharata* than the *Ramayana*.'[5]

Sri Aurobindo suggests that Valmiki knew how to embellish scenes, sentiments, and characters in his poem whereas Vyasa wrote his lines in a matter-of-fact manner, only to convey the essential and never to decorate, not even when he narrated the tragic death of a great hero or the great insult of Draupadi at the hands of the Kauravas. 'Nishkam' (meaning 'without expectation of returns') is the term that Sri Aurobindo uses to describe the style and poetic genius of Vyasa. The couple of keywords used by Rajashekhara[6] and

---

[5]Sri Aurobindo, *The Mahabharata: Essays and Translations*, Pondicherry: Sri Aurobindo Ashram, 1991, 2019, pp. 58–59.

[6]Rajashekhara was a tenth-century literary theorist and a writer who wrote in Sanskrit and an early version of Marathi (the Mahasrashtri Apabhramsha). He is known for his *Kavyamimansa*, a major work on literary theory.

Abhinavagupta[7] respectively, and a single word used by Sri Aurobindo, show how utterly speechless the stupendous epic leaves its spectators or audience. These key terms together also indicate what one should look for in Vyasa's epic.

There are many epics written in various languages from all over the world: *Bayajidda, Eri, Oduduwa, Silamaka,* and *Sundiata* from West Africa and *Lianja* from Central Africa; *Alpamysh* in Turkish; *Bahman Nama, Banu Goshasp Nama, Faramarz Nama,* and *Garshasp Nama* in Persian; *Taghribat Bani Hilal* in Arabic; *The Epic of King Gesar* in Tibetan; *Epic of Gilgamesh,* the oldest epic of the world from Mesopotamia; *Heike Monogatari* in Japanese; *Khamba Thoibi,* a Manipuri epic; *Nagarakertagama* of Indonesia; *Shilappadikaram, Manimekhalai, Jivaka Chintamani, Valayapathi,* and *Kundalakesi* in Tamil; *Beowulf,* an Anglo-Saxon epic written in Old English; *Paradise Lost* and *Paradise Regained* in English; *Iliad* and *Odyssey,* the Ancient Greek epics; *Aeneid,* a Roman epic; *Le Morte d'Arthur,* a collection of Arthurian legends in Middle English; *Judita,* a Croatian epic; *Kalevala,* a Finnish epic; and *Kalevipoeg,* an Estonian epic; among others. Of these, the epics ascribed to Homer set the literary taste and expectations associated with epic poetry with respect to oral epics and John Milton's *Paradise Lost* established the standard for the written epic.

---

[7]Abhinavagupta, from the eleventh century, was probably the ablest literary theorist India produced in the Sanskrit tradition. His *Abhinavabharati* is a classic of great significance for understanding the transition of the Sanskrit literary tradition from the first millennium to the second millennium CE.

Homer's *Odyssey* and Milton's *Paradise Lost* talk about the disconnect between the divine and the human. Homer's hero, Odysseus, wise and gallant, is done with war and ready to go home, but forgets to propitiate Poseidon, the god of the sea, who would provide favourable wind to his sails. This results in a long directionless journey spanning over twelve years. When he arrives home, it is no longer the same. His wife Penelope has almost forgotten her affection for him, though she remembers her duty to him. Many suitors have camped in his city waiting for Penelope to choose one of them as her husband. She has kept them waiting by using a clever ploy of weaving a shroud by day and undoing the stitches at night. When, finally, the protagonist arrives, his son does not recognize him. The story of the Odyssey is about humans enduring the wrath of the gods. After all of his heroic achievements during the war at Troy, Odysseus returns to Ithaca only to realize that he has forever lost the home that he left behind.

The *Iliad* is about the war at Troy, a result of the seduction of Helen by Paris. Prior to the beginning of the love story, the Greek gods are shown as being close to the human protagonists of the tale. At the end of the second epic, however, this connection has snapped altogether. Thus, the two great Greek epics are ultimately the story of how the disconnect between the Greek gods and humans came to be. Homer, to whom the two epics are ascribed, is supposed to have been a blind man. Whether the story of him being blind was made up eighteen centuries after the epics came into circulation, after the English poet John Milton wrote his

Paradise Lost, is a subject for literary scholars to investigate. Milton's two epics, *Paradise Lost* and *Paradise Regained*, at least one of which is remembered as a mighty poem, too convey the theme of the great disconnect. Based on the Biblical myth of loss of the primaeval home of the First Parents—Eve and Adam—in Paradise, the epic narrates how they became victim of Satan's design for destroying God's creation.

The Homeric epics have many alluring episodes. Their plots have the necessary combination of heroism, courage, tragedy, pathos, fantasy, romance, tension, jealousy, caprice, subversion, and supernatural intervention. All the themes that an epic requires are present here; yet, by the early twentieth century, when James Joyce and T. S. Eliot were writing their own masterpieces, the Homeric story had already receded to a kind of mythical past which one could barely recover despite great efforts of imagination. For the generation of the great modernists, if one aligned with myth, one felt alienated from contemporary reality—and if one belonged to contemporary reality, one felt alienated from the past. A great and irreversible disconnect between myth and life had occurred.

Virgil's *Aeneid* was a great poem because it spoke of the beginning of a great empire. Since its time, there has been an unstated assumption that epics are invariably about empire building. Literary critics in the West have often argued that an epic is an extended story that gets written when a great empire, or a great nation, is emerging. At present, however, the greatness of Virgil as a poet remains in the memory of Europe but they have forgotten the greatness of *Aeneid* as a poem. Milton's *Paradise Regained* has been treated from the time it was published, even by his admirers, as a failed attempt. *Paradise Regained* never acquired any life in the imagination of the English literary community, unlike *Paradise Lost*, which exerted a great influence on the imaginations of succeeding generations of poets in England. It became so influential that it would not be an exaggeration to say that Milton managed to destroy the poetic talents of many a poet. John Keats was to say that 'Life to Milton is death to me'.[8] Every major poet of his generation, whether it was Blake, Shelley, Keats, Wordsworth, or Coleridge— known collectively as the Romantic poets—felt Milton's influence and attempted to write their own epics or epical poems. Unfortunately, no one came close to the grandeur of Milton's epic. Keats began *Endymion* but it became a kind of broken dream for him, then he made a second attempt with *Hyperion* but had to abandon it halfway through. Shelley wrote his *Prometheus Unbound,* which tried to celebrate a figure like Milton's Satan. Wordsworth sought to chase his 'lost imagination' through *The Prelude* but had to leave it unfinished. All of them strove to regain the spirit of the epic. But the industrial civilization which had set in did not allow the nineteenth-century British Romantics to write epics. Milton himself, through *Paradise Lost*, recreated the Biblical story of the fall of Man as a conflict between imagination

[8]H. E. Rollins (ed.), *The Letters of John Keats: Vol II, 1819-1821*, Cambridge: Cambridge University Press, 2012.

and reason, and between melancholy and soberness. He was heavily influenced by the prevailing theories in the field of medicine at the time, established by the likes of Richard Burton, who had written his *The Anatomy of Melancholy.*

We notice that in the West the epic form and the epic spirit did not remain accessible to poets after the seventeenth century. Children there have to be consciously *taught* the stories rooted in the Greek or Latin epical tradition in schools. Their myths today come from the Christian or Judaic heritage rather than an epical heritage, whereas in India myths that are still in circulation—the ones shared among a large part of the society, among castes as well as some tribes—and carry forward to the next generation, the ones with which we still sense an organic connection, originate in the *Mahabharata* or the *Ramayana*. They do not come to us from the Vedas or the Upanishads and they do not come from other major works created in ancient India. It is strange but true that the plots and narratives that are commonly circulated in Indian society are not the fictional plots from the *Kathasaritasagara* or the *Vetalapanchisi.* The grip that the *Ramayana* and the *Mahabharata* have over the minds, memories, imaginations, and identities of Indians has no parallel in the literary history in India, or in any other literary tradition. And, in this, the *Mahabharata* has an undisputed pre-eminence over the *Ramayana*. Speaking about the *Mahabharata*, Swami Vivekananda said in 1900:

> In speaking of the *Mahabharata* to you, it is simply impossible for me to present the unending array of

the grand and majestic characters of the mighty heroes depicted by the genius and master-mind of Vyasa. The internal conflicts between righteousness and filial affection in the mind of the god-fearing, yet feeble, old, blind King Dhritarashtra; the majestic character of the grandsire Bhishma; the noble and virtuous character of the royal Yudhishthira, and of the other four brothers, as mighty in valour as in devotion and loyalty; the peerless character of Krishna, unsurpassed in human wisdom; and not less brilliant, the characters of the women— the stately queen Gandhari, the loving mother Kunti, the ever-devoted and all-suffering Draupadi—these and hundreds of other characters of this Epic and those of the *Ramayana* have been the cherished heritage of the whole Hindu world for the last several thousands of years and form the basis of their thoughts and of their moral and ethical ideas.[9]

This is an extraordinary phenomenon and it calls for interpretation and a dispassionate understanding.

It took the scholars at the Bhandarkar Institute in Pune several decades to place this narrative in a sensible textual form by collecting the vast repository of manuscripts from different parts of India, spread over places of traditional learning as apart from each other as Manipur and Madras, Varanasi and Tanjore, Sankheda and Kolkata. They faced the

---

[9]Swami Vivekananda, from the lecture delivered at the Shakespeare Club, Pasadena, California on 1 February 1900, <www.spiritualbee.com/posts/mahabharata-summary-by-swami-vivekananda/>.

complicated task of comparing verse by verse and phrase by phrase the 1,259 handwritten manuscripts, scribed in different centuries and diverse in writing styles and script conventions. Beginning in April 1919, they could complete the project only forty-seven years later, in September 1966, and they produced a printed version of the epic containing 89,000 verses, with notes and editorial comments, with the material excluded from the main text placed in footnotes. The collected, edited, and carefully compared 'critical version' was published in nineteen volumes spread over 15,000 demi-quarto pages. Just as the Kurukshetra war had a series of warriors as generals—Bhishma, Drona, Karna, and Ashwathama—the project had a series of extraordinary editors such as V. S. Sukthankar, S. K. Belvalkar, S. K. De, and R. N. Dandekar. After a lived history of two millennia as a text continuously circulating in the social imagination, the 'original' Sanskrit text of the epic finally came to be consolidated, standardized, authenticated, and brought into print five decades ago. Till then, it remained in existence as an 'oral' epic despite having been first composed by a poet, 'gathered into a larger version' by another poet, 'written' by Ganesha as the myth goes, and reproduced in written manuscripts by generations of scholiasts, as well as translated into several Indian languages and languages from elsewhere in the world, including Persian and English.

Completely unrelated to this project, but during more or less the same period, Sri Aurobindo produced a series of long poems in English based on the *Mahabharata*. His *Love and Death* depicts the Ruru–Priyamvada episode, *Urvasie* is about the story of the Pururavas and Urvashi, and the 24,000-verse-long epic *Savitri* dwells upon the Savitri–Satyavan relationship. His engagement with the epic began in the 1890s and continued till the 1940s.

The number of translations of various parts of the *Mahabharata* and their musical or dramatic representations in Indian languages during medieval times, and more so since printing technology transformed literary productions during the last two hundred years, has been phenomenally large. Four centuries before the critical edition project was launched, the Mughal emperor Akbar had put together a team of poets and scholars to compose a Persian rendering of the epic. The team included Al-Badayuni, who did the first round of the translation, Faizi, Naqib Khan, Mulla Sheri, and a few others who did further work on a few parvas each. Akbar commissioned artists to illustrate the manuscript and titled the translation *Razmnama*, the history of a war. The illustrations depicted events from the *Mahabharata* as well as the *Ramayana*. It appears that some of the artists retrenched by Akbar went out to the Agra bazaar and sold their unused paintings. Some of these may be seen in a publication put together by Ashok Kumar Das in 1985, called *Paintings of the Razmnama: The Book of War*.

Translations of the *Mahabharata* into Tamil were carried out as early as the ninth century by the poet Perundevanar, under the title *Bharat Venba*, and, later in the fourteenth century, by Villiputhurar. The Telugu *Mahabharata*, the first great literary work synchronous with the birth of the Telugu language, was composed by Nannaya in the eleventh century.

The phenomenal Narayanappa, who came to be recognized as Kumar Vyasa, a poet of great literary prowess, produced the Kannada version of the *Mahabharata*. Several episodes from the *Mahabharata* were translated frequently into other languages, for instance, Gujarati and Bangla. So far, there have been no attempts to collect all such translations in full length or abridged versions for a comprehensive comparison. As and when that is accomplished, it will become possible to know more about the original *Mahabharata* as it exactly was, and to understand more fully the history of its cultural impact.

In addition to the translations available in Indian languages and the 'critical edition' in Sanskrit, there exists living oral *Mahabharata* compositions in various tribal languages. One such work is the long poem *Bharath* in the Garasiya variety of Bhili spoken in the Banaskantha–Sabarkantha area on the border of Rajasthan and Gujarat. A dedicated schoolteacher with a doctorate in folk literature, Bhagwandas Patel from Banaskantha spent several decades documenting the text and the performance practices of the Bhils' *Bharath*. His text is now available in Gujarati, Hindi, and English versions. The plot of the *Mahabharata* of the Garasiya Bhils and the plot in the 'critical edition' *Mahabharata* have shared elements, but the differences are quite striking. For instance, the vastra haran, disrobing of Draupadi, does not occur in the tribal epic. As against the sarpa yagnya in the 'critical edition', the tribal text depicts Vasuki, the king of serpents, as being far more heroic and triumphant than any of the Kuru heroes. In the Bhili version, Vasuki has a romping affair with Draupadi, and Arjuna is depicted as a mute spectator tied to the bedpost while Vasuki and Draupadi are in bed.[10] There is no *Bhagavad Gita* in the tribal epic, though Krishna as a character, and an important one, is present. Neither the Satyavan–Savitri story, nor the Nala–Damayanti story, and not even the Ruru–Pramadvara story are to be found in the Bhili *Mahabharata*. The rituals associated with its recitation and performance clearly indicate that the Bhili *Mahabharata* belongs to the realm of the sacred in their culture.

My idea of what an oral epic is, or can be, is shaped by the Bhili *Mahabharata*. I have read the documented text carefully and seen it performed several times. I have also spoken to the members of the community, who undertake years of training to perform the epic. It is clear to me that theirs is not a 'vulgarization' or a folk adaptation of the *Mahabharata*. It is more likely to be an earlier version of the epic, in existence prior to the compendious and inclusive corpus prepared by Vyasa some two millennia ago, free of the erotic portions of the narrative not relevant to the main story.

There are other such versions of the *Mahabharata* in existence in India. Besides, there are the *Bhagavad* and the *Gita* and, together, they continue to keep the *Mahabharata* tradition alive in India. Indians, old or young, in cities or in villages, think that they know the *Mahabharata* although they rarely read the poem in print. There is a widely shared

---

[10]See Nila Shah (trans.), *Bharath: An Epic of the Dungri Bhils*, documented by Bhagwandas Patel, Baroda: Bhasha Centre and Central Institute of Indian Languages, 2012.

superstition that it is inauspicious to keep copies of the entire text at home. No such taboo is attached to the *Bhagavad Gita*, and its copies are acquired and kept in homes. Most Indians in urban and semi-urban areas watch the *Mahabharata* on the TV screen, and many listen to oral renderings of some of the main episodes. Till the early twentieth century, the tradition of reciting verses from the *Mahabharata* during winter months continued in most parts of rural India. During the last few decades, the votaries of oral epic traditions have become rare. At present, one's access to the epic has become somewhat reduced. Children are introduced to it through illustrated storybooks, and adults get to 'see' it enacted on the TV screen. And yet, we like to believe that we know the *Mahabharata*. No other imaginative composition, no other literary work except perhaps the *Ramayana*, has held so much sway over such vast numbers and over such a long time span. No other epic anywhere in the world has so substantially been an integral part of a people's emotional life as this epic.

It is said that an epic is a poem of a century. That, perhaps, should be an understatement. Epics do not get written every century. Not all poems written as epics, even if they are very long, necessarily acquire the status of an epic. Most of Western mythology originates with the *Iliad* and the *Odyssey*, though a different order of Western mythology originates in the Biblical tradition. Over the last three centuries, as I have argued, Western modernity has eclipsed Homeric mythology to a great extent. That has not been the case with the *Mahabharata*. Similarly, Virgil's *Aeneid* and Dante's *Divine Comedy*, though they continue to be revered as classics, no longer have a living presence in the imagination of modern Western nations. John Milton's *Paradise Lost* exists today only as a classroom text for students of literature, and even they do not usually read the companion epic *Paradise Regained*.

Sri Aurobindo spent nearly four decades working on his *Savitri*, and Vinayak Krishna Gokak composed a poem intended to be an epic, *Bharata Sindhu Rashmi*, in Kannada. While in literary circles these poems are seen as significant texts, they did not acquire the status of epics in the minds of the common readers in India. Howsoever large, experimental, challenging, and aesthetically pleasing they may be, such poems fall short of becoming epic. It would, therefore, be realistic to maintain that the length of a poem alone cannot qualify it as an epic. An epic, instead, is a poem that emerges at the beginning of a civilization and becomes an icon for that civilization. A new civilization is not just the arrival of a new social class in the position of dominance or only the ascendence of a new literary sensibility. A civilization springs up when a pervasive epistemic change starts taking place, a change fundamentally altering people's perspectives on material, cultural, and spiritual matters.

The *Mahabharata* tells us about the change taking place in ancient India over an extended period of time, spanning several centuries. But, if it does so, what indeed was the nature of the epistemic change that interested the *Mahabharata*? Irawati Karve, a respected cultural anthropologist, describes the *Mahabharata* in her fascinating book *Yuganta* as a depiction of the end of an era, a shift from the pastoral–agrarian state system to an early feudal state structure in India. A poem recording such a major shift in a prehistoric time should obviously be seen as a substitute for history and invite the interest of generations into that grey area in India's history. The drive to know or imagine the point of origin dominates people's imagination in all civilizations and all ages. But is there something else, and equally fundamental, implied in the epic's continuing influence on people, and in Indian society's engagement with the epic? Is there something in the nation–epic relationship that the *Mahabharata* strikes that has escaped the attention of its critics? That too is a question requiring our attention.

Commentators and literary scholars in the past have usually depended on linguistic and archaeological evidence while dealing with the *Mahabharata* question. Astronomy and mathematics too have been used by a few commentators on ancient Indian texts. Bal Gangadhar Tilak's *The Orion*, published during the last decade of the nineteenth century, argues that since Bhishma's death is reported to have taken place in the month of Magha, the war may have taken place during an era when 'the winter solstice must have coincided in those days with the beginning of Dhanishtha as described in the *Vedanga Jyotisha* and other works'.[11] He quotes in support verse 169 of the *Anushasana Parva*. Since then, Tilak's calculations and the logic of his argument have been disputed and rejected by most historians.

The rulers and dynasties known to have existed in ancient

---

[11]Bal Gangadhar Tilak, *The Orion: Or Researches into the Antiquity of the Vedas*, Pune: Geeta Printers, 1893, 1999, p. 29.

India in the grey zone between prehistory and history are the Pradyota dynasty (682–544 BCE), Haryanka dynasty (544–413 BCE), Shishunaga dynasty (413–345 BCE), Nanda dynasty (345–321 BCE), and the Maurya dynasty (321–185 BCE). Barring the early occurrence of script and writing practices in the Indus Valley civilization (4400–3900 BP), which has not been deciphered yet, the earliest known use of script for writing language known in India is to be found in the Edicts of Ashoka from 2250 BP.[12] Since the fully formed script would require a significant amount of time for its emergence and spread, it is likely that writing was known only in limited circles before this date. Some of the inscriptions such as the Barli pillar inscription and Sohgaura copper plate inscription are thought to belong to a slightly earlier period, though the instances of any formal use of script do not date back to the times prior to the reign of Ashoka. It is interesting to note that Panini 'wrote' his famous *Ashtadhyayi* during the 5–6 BCE, or even earlier. Various Western and Indian scholars have placed him between twenty-four and twenty-seven centuries before us. This goes to show that 'writing' which we can access was indeed possible and practised by ancient Indian scholars at least since twenty-five centuries ago.

In the tradition of Indian literature, leaving aside literature carried forward entirely through oral traditions, the author of the epic *Ramayana* is considered through a universal

---

[12]BP is Before Present. It makes it easier for a reader to visualise the past without getting into the complexities of counting as required in BCE (Before Common Era).

consensus to be the first poet. His *Ramayana*, consisting of 24,000 shlokas, is usually dated around first century BCE, at a conservative estimate, and around third century BCE, in a generous estimate. The *Mahabharata* was *written* a little later than the *Ramayana*, as the impact of Valmiki's style can be easily detected in Vyasa's poetic style. It is probable, and one can only say 'probable', that a poet known as Vyasa *wrote* the *Mahabharata* around 3–1 BCE, or even slightly later. However, this 'writing' was not exactly completely 'original'. The corpus he created contained an earlier orally transmitted epic written by a certain Krishna Dwaipayana and several other narratives. These included the tales of Nala and Damayanti, Savitri and Satyavan, Ruru and Pramadvara, and so on. He also seems to have added to the previously existing oral narratives and incorporated in his work a vast legacy of 'remembrances of things past',[13] beginning with the early Vedic era to the war at Kurukshetra.

The Kurukshetra war appears to have taken place prior to the emergence of the Pradyota dynasty. This dynasty had formed a strong regime some twenty-eight centuries before our time. Preceding the Pradyotas, India's prehistory mentions the Kurus,[14] who appear to have been in existence for nearly four centuries, around twenty-nine to thirty-two

---

[13]Original English title of Marcel Proust's *In Search of Lost Time*.

[14]Apart from the *Mahabharata*—which is all about the Kuru war—the Kurus find mention in every book on India's prehistory. See, for instance: Michael Witzel, 'Early Sanskritization: Origin and Development of the Kuru State', *Electronic Journal of Vedic Studies (EJVS)*, Vol. 1, No. 4, 1995, pp. 1–26.

centuries before our time. The Great War at Kurukshetra, therefore, was fought probably thirty centuries ago, given that we have evidence of a few generations of Kuru kings in power even after the epic war. The long narrative composed initially, albeit in oral form, may have come into existence immediately following the war, maybe twenty-eight centuries ago, and the larger *Mahabharata* corpus may have come into existence and been committed to writing in some form nine or ten centuries after the previously existing narrative(s) began circulating. The practice of reciting the *Bharata*[15], and later the *Mahabharata,* is likely to have been widespread; and the more its spread, the greater the chances of new additions to the larger corpus, the *Maha*Bharata. In tune with the tradition upon which Vyasa built his epic, the text composed by him was carried forward orally, generation to generation and continued to acquire new material and additions along its trajectory through centuries. The *Gita*, it is believed, is one such later addition. So is the sublimation of the character of Krishna and his status as an Avatar. Perhaps, the coexistence of the *Ramayana* and the *Mahabharata* in the public sphere, not guarded by Vedic Brahminism, may be the reason for the idea of the Avatar gaining circulation and wide acceptance during the first millennium after Christ. The larger text making it *Mahabharata*, and the practice of cultural remembrance, spread all over in the country and

---

[15]Having approximately 24,000 verses, this version was much shorter than the epic we now know as the *Mahabharata,* and which was described as Jaya (victory or conquest) or Itihasa (history) or Jaya-Itihasa.

across non-Brahminical classes over the last two thousand years, with some parts of the poem gaining a greater urgency at one time, and other parts gaining traction at others. In the entire range of literature produced in the early phases of ancient India—the Vedas, Upanishads, Vedangas, Brahmans, Smritis, and Shastras—the *Ramayana* and the *Mahabharata* alone enjoyed a free circulation among all classes of society and were, somewhat ambivalently, exempted from the strict pollution rules of the time. They became, therefore, substitutes for the dharmagranthas for those who were denied direct access to the 'sacred' texts of ancient India. The *Mahabharata*, with its greater variety and complexity of characters, remained the most popular text in the genres of history-of-a-kind and imaginative literature for most Indians. It appears to have played this unique cultural role for the last thirty centuries, first in its shorter bardic form and later in Vyasa's compendious *written* epic, albeit carried forward mainly through the oral tradition, and finally through its episodic rendering in theatre, dance, and music. Its translations to modern Indian languages aided this spread.

In recent years, genetics has produced some new evidence on the question of the ethnic composition of India during ancient times. For those who are interested in following this method, I would like to recommend a recent work by David Reich, *Who We Are and How We Got Here.* Reich reports genetic research available up to 2016, and based on the findings of various research teams, he offers provisional inferences and some speculations about the origins of the people of India and the prehistoric periods of their spread. There are, of course, risks involved in using genetics to describe a society as, if applied tendentiously, it can be easily drawn towards supporting racist and casteist theories. Reich himself is aware of the danger. Therefore, he opens his discussion of India by commenting on how Adolf Hitler used the linguistic research available to him to support the theory of the Western conquest of India and floated the Aryan myth and the uses of symbols like the swastika. Without overlooking the risk, it would be worth looking at what genetics has to say about the 'past' as it would have been understood by Indians some thirty centuries before our time.

Reich's interest in India was triggered, as he tells us, by 'a book and a letter'.[16] The book was Luigi Luca Cavalli-Sforza's *The History and Geography of Human Genes*. It contains a hypothesis about the Negrito people of Andaman, who, if research would corroborate, can provide details of the 'Out of Africa' people who arrived there some 40,000 years ago. In order to carry out this research, Reich got in touch with Lalji Singh and Kumaraswamy Thangaraj, scientists working at Hyderabad's Centre for Cellular and Molecular Biology. The Indian scientists, in turn, decided to involve Reich and his colleague Nick Patterson. The team of four worked on a large pool of gene samples to study the DNA, matching them with the purpose of determining the exact nature of the 'mix' of population in India over the last 9,000 years. They moved

---

[16]David Reich, *Who We Are and How We Got Here: Ancient DNA and the New Science of the Human Past*, New York: Pantheon Books, 2018, p. 128.

from hypothesis to hypothesis, built them and knocked them down as new evidence and research tools became available to them. Their primary aim was to see when exactly the southern people mixed with the northern people. I shall not go over the entire trajectory of development of their final conclusions. Let me bring here the final findings, which too may get further refined as this field of research develops over the coming decades. There are still some conspicuous gaps in the world's knowledge of the exact history of the Indian population, mainly arising out of the absence of complete information about the Harappa people.

> The picture of population movement in India is still far less crisp than our picture of Europe because of the lack of ancient DNA from South Asia. An outstanding mystery is the ancestry of the peoples of the Indus Valley Civilization, who were spread across the Indus Valley and parts of the northern India between forty-five hundred to thirty-eight hundred years ago, and were at the crossroads of all these great ancient movements of people.[17]

Three possibilities were explored in 2015: a) Were they a mix of the agriculturalists from Iran and the Ancestral South Indians (ASI); b) Were they a mix of the agriculturalists from Iran and the Ancestral North Indians (ANI); or c) Were they Iranian agrarians? Answers to these questions will take time. But, till then, what we know about the great mix of peoples

---

[17]Ibid., pp. 152–53.

in India, leaving out the Indus Valley civilization, is as follows.

Human population in India goes back to some 40,000 years as the population was expanding in Eurasia 50,000 years ago. India received agriculture from two sources. Eurasian agriculture came via Iran to the Indus Valley some 9,000 years ago, spreading from there to the northern parts of India, bringing with it the Near Eastern winter rainfall crops of wheat and barley. The local population adapted these to the rainfall conditions in India. On the other hand, the Chinese rainfall crops of rice and millet reached India approximately 5,000 years ago. The Harappa culture and civilization prospered between 2500–1700 BCE, and perished for reasons still not fully determined. This was the time when the Eurasian people started moving to the western frontiers of India. These people had, before moving, developed a language, now known as Indo-Iranian, that also migrated west towards Iran. The linguistic split took almost a thousand years. By that time, the branch that had been slowly moving towards India became independent. This branch is the one that we know as the Indo Aryan. They inherited the Yamnaya civilization, evidenced through archaeological excavations at Sintashta, Potapovka, and Arkaim, and brought it to India in a substantially reformed shape.

The era covering their slow movement is known in Indian history as the Vedic Age. It is during this period, and some centuries following this time, that a new mixing and the resultant clash of peoples took place in India. All of that is intimately related to the substance, form, and meaning of the *Mahabharata*. In David Anthony's landmark study, *The Horse,*

The Wheel, and Language, of how the use of horse-driven cars with two axel wheels changed the history of humankind, he refers to Lubotsky's etymological study and comments:

> The Old Indic of the *Rig Veda* contained at least 383 non-Indo-European words borrowed from a source belonging to a different language family. Alexander Lubotsky has shown that common Indo-Iranian, the parent of both Old Indic and Iranian, probably had already borrowed words from the same non-Indo-European words that later enriched Old Indic. He compiled a list of 55 non-Indo-European words that were borrowed into common Indo-Iranian *before* Old Indic or Avestan evolved, and then later was inherited into one or both of the daughters from common Indo-Iranian. The speakers of common Indo-Iranian were in touch with and borrowed terms from *the same foreign language group* that later was the source from which Old Indic speakers borrowed even more terms.[18]

The borrowed words included Indra, Soma, homa (sacred fire), nagna (bread), and sphara (ploughshare). Old Indic, the earliest known form of Sanskrit, was formed between 1500 BCE and 1300 BCE. The earliest layers of the language found in the Vedas belong to this period. The later layers of the Vedic language emerged some twenty-eight to thirty-two

---

[18]David W. Anthony, *The Horse, the Wheel, and Language: How Bronze-Age Riders from the Eurasian Steppes Shaped the Modern World*, Princeton and Oxford: Princeton University Press, 2007, p. 455.

centuries before us. It was not just the language that came to India and started interacting with the languages and peoples who had knowledge of agriculture and house building. With them came the horse-driven fast cart, the chariot. The chariot people, the speakers of the Old Indic, brought with them the traces of what the Yamnaya culture had gathered along its long journey through a millennium—the deities, forms of worship, male predominance in sacred affairs, and the faith in word as an abstract power. David Anthony writes:

> The people of the Rig Veda did not live in brick houses, and had no cities, although their enemies, the Dasyus, did live in walled strongholds. Chariots were used in races and war; the gods drove chariots across the sky. Almost all important deities were masculine. The only important female deity was Dawn, and she was less powerful than Indra, Varuna, Mitra, Agni, or the Divine Twins (Ashwins).[19]

Given the explicit use of Vedic deities in the *Mahabharata* story, and the numerous tales describing the destruction of various kingdoms, the sarpa yagna[20]—and the existence of a city such as Dwarka and involvement of kings from the south and east—it is probable that the *Mahabharata* was trying to encapsulate the entire past from the times of the early contact of the horse-driven chariot-riding pastoral people

---

[19]Ibid., p. 456.

[20]The sarpa (serpent/snake) yagna (sacrifice) is an important part of the plot of the *Mahabharata* epic. It appears in the early portion of the story.

and the agrarian city-building people of India to the times when the practice of reciting the *Bharata* emerged in the ashrams. Both the chariot-driving early Vedic people and the *Bharata*-reciting latter-day 'historians' have their marks inscribed in the text-corpus of the *Mahabharata*.

In a remarkable pointer to the amount of historical memory that the *Mahabharata* contains, the closing point of the story brings us back straight to the starting point, separated by several centuries, probably a millennium or so. David Anthony writes that the Srubnaya site excavated by him revealed the mid-winter solstice ceremony of the times when the Proto-Indo-Iranian was in use, a sacrifice site where nearly 40 per cent bones found were of dogs. The winter solstice ceremony was associated in that era with the initiation of the young into the warrior category and 'the principle symbol was dog or wolf. Dogs represented death; multiple dogs or multiple headed dog (*Cerberus, Saranyu*) guarded the entrance of the Afterworld.'[21] This symbolism in use some thirty-eight centuries before our time is invoked in the *Mahabharata* probably a thousand years later. Dharmaraja, known during his life as Yudhishthira, enters the world of Yama with a dog accompanying him. On his insistence, the dog too is allowed to come up to the Gate of the Afterworld and further. The philosophical and metaphysical understanding of death and cremation rituals had changed remarkably between the times of Yamnaya and the time of the composition of the *Bharata*. The culture of

---

[21]Anthony, *The Horse, the Wheel, and Language*, p. 411.

remembrance had not. The method of presenting history and the past as it was in terms of myth and myth as if it were an organic part of the people's past makes them temporally distant but organically linked parts of a historiography.

The great remembrance was the *Bharata*, and the one who is believed to have brought all the hundreds of stories, characters, events, beliefs, and moods together is believed to be Vyasa, or a Krishna Dwaipayana. When did this poet decide to reconstruct the past as he saw it? Why? And how did he gather the multitude of sagas into a single string of stories? These are intriguing questions, and answering them can be an intellectual adventure. But, before attempting that, I would like to return to genetics once again, for this branch of human study can lead one to conclusions that can easily be misused for arriving at socially disastrous conclusions if not used cautiously.

While studying the Indian people, Reich noticed that there are innumerable 'clans' in India marked by endogamy in their personal life but who connect with others in economic activities. 'Caste' is the term used for such clans. On studying the origin of some of these communities, he noticed that due to their strict marriage rules, it was relatively easier to trace their genetic history. He called them 'population bottlenecks', a term that linguistics as well as anthropology commonly uses for people born into a single family continuing to retain their family identity over a long time. One such 'population bottleneck' found, and closely studied using modern laboratory techniques, was the Vyasa community. Reich observes:

One of the most striking things we discovered was in the Vyasa of the southern Indian state of Andhra Pradesh, a middle caste group of approximately five million people whose population bottleneck we could date (from the size of segments shared between individuals of the same population) to between three thousand and two thousand years ago.

The observation of such a strong population bottleneck among the ancestors of the Vyasa was shocking. It meant that after the population bottleneck, the ancestors of Vyasa had maintained strict endogamy, allowing essentially no genetic mixing into their group for thousands of years. Even an average rate of influx into the Vyasa of as little as one percent per generation, would have erased the genetic signal of a population bottleneck. The ancestors of Vyasa did not live in geographical isolation. Instead they lived cheek by jowl with other groups in a densely populated part of India. Despite proximity to other groups, the endogamy rules and group identity in the Vyasa have been so strong that they maintained strict social isolation from their neighbours....[22]

The ideas of endogamy, purity of the family line, and associated sense of responsibility are stated boldly in the first chapter of the *Gita*, which has come to be seen as an essential component of the *Mahabharata*:

---

[22]Reich, *Who We Are and How We Got Here*, p. 144.

Kulakshaye pranashyanti kuldharma sanatanah
Dharma nashte kilam krutstram dharmo abhibhavatyut

From the ruin of the family are totally destroyed the
traditional rites and duties of the family.
When rites and duties are destroyed, vice overpowers
the entire family also.[23]

It would probably be a pointless chase to see if the South
Indian Vyasa community that has preserved its genetic
identity through strict endogamy over the last 3,000 years
and the Vyasa, or the Krishna of the Dark Island, who is
accepted as the prime narrator of the *Mahabharata* has any
connection to the community.

It would also be futile to ask if the strong statement
by Arjuna at the beginning of the *Gita* against kula kshaya,
degeneration of clan purity, is the author's idea or the
thoughts of someone like him. There simply is no evidence
available, nor will it ever become available, to ascertain
this. Yet, it would not be too off the mark to propose that
the poet of the *Mahabharata* was someone belonging to a
'middle caste', neither a Brahmin like the Acharyas of the
Mahabharata nor like the Kshatriya warriors involved in the
epic war. The *Adi Parva*, sarga 62, states:

The history of the exalted birth of the *Bharata* princes
is called the *Mahabharata*. He who knoweth this
etymology of the name is cleansed of all his sins. And

---

[23]Swami Gambhirananda (trans.), *Bhagavad Gita: With the Commentary
of Shankaracharya,* Kolkata: Swapna, 1991, I. 40, p. 26.

as this history of the Bharata race is so wonderful, that, when recited, it assuredly purifieth mortals from all sins. The sage Krishna-Dwaipayana completed his work in three years. Rising daily and purifying himself and performing his ascetic devotions, he composed this *Mahabharata*. Therefore, this should be heard by Brahmanas with the formality of a vow. He who reciteth this holy narration composed by Krishna for the hearing of others, and they who hear it, in whatever state he or they may be, can never be affected by the fruit of deeds, good or bad. The man desirous of acquiring virtue should hear it all. This is equivalent to all histories....[24]

The 'great remembrance' that the *Mahabharata* is, in all probability, the construction of history from a third point of view, of a sakshi, a sthitpragnya, an observer who was neither wonderstruck by the advent of the charioteers nor thrilled by the great city-building agrarian princes. This hypothesis offers to us a different view of the *Mahabharata*, and some useful insights into the development of the Indian people during the period extending from the post-Harappan period to the times of Gautama Buddha, from forty-four centuries BP to twenty-five centuries BP before our time. Commenting on Vyasa's style, Sri Aurobindo wrote, 'Vyasa's art, as I have said, is singularly disinterested "*nishkam*"; he does not write with a view to sublimity or with a view to beauty, but because

---

[24]K. M. Ganguli (trans.), *The Mahabharata of Krishna-Dwaipayana Vyasa: translated into English Prose from the Original Sanskrit Text,* Kolkata: Bharata Press, 1883–1896.

he has certain ideas to impart, certain events to describe, certain characters to portray. He has an image of these in his mind and his business is to find an expression for it which will be scrupulously just to his conception.'[25]

Epics, by nature of their scope and placement at the beginning of a new civilization or a new era, are normally seen as a statement of the 'unconscious metaphysics of their time'.[26] The *Mahabharata*, though suffused in full measure with ideas and utterances from the Vedas and the early Upanishads, appears to be stating a metaphysics that is not peculiarly Vedic. Lest this observation is misunderstood, let me elaborate. The vehicle for articulating the metaphysics of the day, various epics have used two great literary devices. The first is the use of the supernatural and the second is the elaborate debates evaluating philosophical positions and existential choices. The former is brought in by using mythic elements, the latter by setting up war assemblies. Myth is in the making of the *Mahabharata* what bones are to a body. Its presence is so seminal in the progress of the plot that the audiences of the *Mahabharata* easily tend to think the poem is all about myths. The war debates, too, and the oracles, are several but the most important 'war debate' in the *Mahabharata* is the composition known the world over as the *Bhagavad Gita*. A comment on both will offer us a better view of the metaphysics of the day that the

---

[25]Aurobindo, *The Mahabharata*, p. 42.
[26]E. M. W. Tillyard, *The English Epic and its Background,* New York: Barnes & Noble, 1966, p. 113.

Mahabharata brings into the poem. Let us first consider the principal war debate in the epic and then turn to the mythic element and the presence of the supernatural.

The Great War debate appears in the *Bhagavad Gita*, a text of extraordinary sublimity, placed in the *Bhishma Parva*, the book that narrates the commencement of the war. Of the forty cantos of the *Bhishma Parva*, eighteen are occupied by the debate between Arjuna and Krishna, with Krishna occupying the most space. These are cantos 23 to 40. These cantos are now known as the eighteen adhyayas, chapters, of the *Gita*. The numerical symmetry cannot be easily overlooked. In an epic with eighteen parvas, depicting an eighteen-day war, there is the debate occupying eighteen cantos. There is an inconclusive debate as to the *Gita* being originally a part of the epic. But, no matter when in later history it was so seamlessly woven into the epic-text, and by whom, there is not an iota of doubt that the numerical symmetry of the eighteen adhyayas for an epic with eighteen parvas is intended to foreground the *Gita* as the crucially defining feature of the *Mahabharata*.

Without digressing too much into historical research, it would be useful for us to know that the language register used in the *Bhagavad Gita* and its diction point to it being a composition of the post-Panini period, which made use of 'na' to denote negation as a parallel and substitute to the 'ma' used in Sanskrit compositions prior to Panini. Thus, while Krishna chastises Arjuna, asking him to not be plunged into gloom—*klaibyam ma sma gama Partha*—he also assures him that even when the body is lost, the soul remains unaffected by the elements of fire, water, and wind: *nainam chhndanti shastrani, nainamdahati pavakah; na chainam kledayntapo, na shoshayati marutah.*[27] The uncertainty about the date of its composition and incorporation into the epic is neither more nor less in degree than the uncertainty about the date of composition of the epic itself. We shall discuss this later. However, it is necessary to consider the relatively late arrival of Lord Krishna in the Hindu pantheon. He was not part of the Vedic pantheon, which gave primacy to Surya, Indra, Varuna, and Agni. Similarly, the darshanas, schools of ancient and classical Indian philosophy, do not mention Krishna in any major discussion.

Towards the end of the first millennium, about eleven centuries before our time, Adi Shankara prepared a massive commentary on the *Gita,* the *Gita Bhashya.* Since then, during the last thousand years, Krishna as a deity rose in eminence among the medieval sects. This was reflected in iconography, theatre, dance, painting, music, and literature. The Vaishnava Acharyas, Ramanuja and Madhava, gave the *Bhagavad Gita* centrality in their philosophical expositions. Poets like Jayadeva composed the *Gita Govinda* with lyrics of haunting charm on the life of Krishna. Religious rituals related to Krishna emerged and were consolidated as large mass events. Apparently secular community festivals such as the Raas dance during Navaratri and Holi placed Krishna at the heart of the celebrations. A great poet like

---

[27]Swami Gambhirananda (trans.), *Bhagavad Gita: With the Commentary of Shankaracharya*, Kolkata: Swapna, 1991, pp. 2–23.

Mira composed immortal poems pining for Krishna. The continued engagement with the *Gita* reached its high during the twentieth century. Major social, cultural, and spiritual leaders alluded to it, wrote about it, translated it, and offered compendious commentaries. These include Swami Vivekananda, Lokmanya Tilak, Sri Aurobindo, Mahatma Gandhi, Vinoba Bhave, and Sarvepalli Radhakrishnan. In modern India, the *Gita* has acquired a special status as a definitive religious text by being accorded legitimacy in law courts by the legal system. It is a text accepted for taking oaths.

As we have seen, the *Mahabharata* emerged in ancient India as an oral epic. The *Gita*, placed within it at some stage in its historical journey, has come to be its representation and is accepted as *the* written text for people who formally identify as being Hindu. Just as it is difficult to say if the *Gita* of Krishna was originally a part of the *Mahabharata*, it is also difficult to say if the great devotion to the *Gita* in the second millennium of Indian history was because it was a part of the epic, or whether the undiminished popularity of the *Mahabharata* till this day has been a result of the *Gita* being a part of it. And yet, one can be certain beyond any doubt that the essence of the *Gita*—the precept of detachment, and the perspective of an uninvolved witness, the sthitpragnya or sakshi—was the precise sentiment that the *Mahabharata* epic sought to evoke in the minds of its audiences.

The epic has received unceasing attention throughout its existence for the last twenty and more centuries; but the most precise description of the poem and its poetic effect was, I like to think, by the eleventh century scholar-philosopher Abhinavagupta. After commenting at length on the *Mahabharata* and the *Gita*, he concluded that the rasa (poetic sentiment) that the *Mahabharata* evokes in the minds of the rasikas (literary audience) is to be called 'shanta'. Here, it must be noted that the dramatist Bharata who had formulated the Rasa theory a millennium before Abhinava had classified rasas into eight types, such as sringara rasa, vira rasa, etc. However, he had not conceptualized the shanta rasa. Abhinavagupta coined the term, proposed the concept, and applied it to the *Mahabharata*. Abhinavagupta described shanta rasa thus:

> Because śānta is common to all *rasas*, it would be improper to name especially a colour or god that is appropriate to it, as one has done for the other *rasas*, but they have been invented by some. And so the reasonableness of śānta has been shown. Its true nature is *hāsya*. *Vīra* and *bibhatsa* tend to lead towards it. Therefore there is in the case of śānta the advice about the practice of *yama*, *niyama*, meditation on God, etc. It stands to reason that it leads to a great result (i.e., *mokṣa*), as it eschews enjoyment of worldly objects (*anupabhogitayā*), that it is more important than any other *rasa*, and that it pervades the entire plot. And so enough of further elaboration.
>
> What is the nature of its true relish? It is the following: The nature of the soul is tinged by *utsāha*, *rati*, etc., which are capable of imparting their peculiar

tinges to it. It is like a very white thread that shines through the interstices of sparsely threaded jewels. It assumes the forms of all the various feelings like love, etc., which are superimposed on it, because all these things are capable of importing their tinges to it. Even then (*tathābhāvenāpi*) it shines out through them, according to the maxim that once this Ātman shines, it shines forever. It is devoid of the entire collection of miseries which consist in (i.e., which result from) turning away from the *Ātman*. It is identical with the consciousness of the realisation of the highest bliss. It takes its effect through the process of generalisation in poetry and drama. It makes such a heart (i.e., the heart of the sensitive spectator or reader) the receptacle of an other-worldly bliss by inducing a peculiar kind of introspection (*antarmukhāvasthābheda*).[28]

The unconscious metaphysics that the epic *Mahabharata* aims at articulating is the metaphysics of shanta, and the metaphysics of being a sthitpragnya, a sakshi. If the origin of the *Mahabharata* was in its desire to narrate the social composition of ancient India beginning with the early Vedic period till the start of the historical period, chronologically somewhere close to the times of Gautama Buddha, if the subject of the epic was the depiction of a greatly destructive war, if the plot of the poem was suffused with the tragic loss of heroes and princesses of great mental and physical

---

[28]Abhinavagupta, *Abhinavabhārati*, J. L. Masson and M. V. Patwardhan (trans.), Delhi: Motilal Banarsidass, 1971, pp. 239–40.

qualities, yet the impact it sought to make on the readers was of an empathetic detachment, not a cold-blooded retreat but a sage acceptance of all that has been as it was. The word in Sanskrit that can most aptly describe this philosophic resignation would be 'itihasa', or this is how it has been. However, the *Mahabharata* was not like a Greek tragedy, intended for the catharsis of the minds of the spectators, nor like the Greek epics—despite many shared elements—intended for creating a great admiration for the hero, or rather heroes. Rajashekhara, a remarkable literary critic, poet, and dramatist, has left for us a timeless piece of advice some eleven centuries ago. He remarked that when one speaks of the *Ramayana*, one speaks of a single hero; but speaking of the *Mahabharata*, one speaks 'of many heroes'.[29] 'Shanta rasa' and 'many heroes'—these four words take us to the very heart of what the *Mahabharata* has been.

THE ENDLESS PLOT

The structural unity of a literary work is generally described by referring to the elements that run through it from the beginning to the very end and the ones that keep making appearances during the action and narration at key points in the plot. If it is an epic or a tragedy, unity can also be defined in terms of the pervasive presence of a heroic character throughout the plot, a character that dominates the action and the story. In the case of the *Mahabharata*, it would be

---

[29]G. N. Devy, *Of Many Heroes: An Indian Essay on Literary Historiography*, Delhi: Orient Blackswan, 1998, p. 17.

difficult to say who the central character is. There have been numerous studies of this epic and poetic and fictional works inspired by it in Indian languages, as well as in English and other languages, trying to present either Arjuna, Karna, Krishna, Bhishma, Kunti, or Draupadi as the key character in the action. A mere list of such works could fill a book. Yet, if one were to match these claims with the structure of the epic, there appears to be difficulties and exceptions that can hardly be set aside. Bhishma, who is present in the story from its early stages, if not from the very beginning, does not stay in it to the very end. Both Karna and Krishna appear at a much later stage and are not present till the end. Draupadi's claim as the most central character is a little more tenable since she is present at most of the crucial turning points of the plot and is in it till almost the very end. However, her role in the plot is probably just as important as that of Sita in the *Ramayana*, neither more nor less. Just as the *Ramayana* is about Sita, but more importantly about something else, the *Mahabharata* is about something much more than the plight of Draupadi, though her plight becomes one of the causes for the war eventually fought. The expanse and the grandeur of the action and the heroic qualities of the major characters of the *Mahabharata* are so dazzling that, surprisingly, one tends to overlook the fact that the one character who is present at the very beginning as well as the very end is Yama. He is also present in the action, in all its crucial active and contemplative moments.

Yama, in popular imagination, is associated with death. He is imagined to be the sovereign of the land to which the dead depart. But that was not how Yama was positioned in ancient myths. In the pre-*Mahabharata* mythology, Yama is described as Time as well as Light. In the *Rig Veda*, dated by scholars prior to the era of the *Mahabharata*, Yama is the son of Vivasvan and Saranya. Vivasvan is himself the Sun God and Saranya is the Goddess of Dusk. At this juncture in the evolution of Indian myths, Yama was not yet seen as the God of Death. He was an immortal who opted to undergo death. In that sense, he is the first to be both a mortal and an immortal being. He combines light and darkness in his person, given his parentage. Students of comparative literature will find a fertile field for research if they compare this ideation with the great intellectual struggle that ancient Greeks had to undertake for correlating substance and its shadow. Yama had a sister named Yami. The two names are similar as both words are respectively the male and female terms for 'twin'. The following conversation between them forms one of the subsections, sukta, of a chapter in the *Rig Veda*:

1. FAIN would I win my friend to kindly friendship. So may the Sage, come through the air's wide ocean, Remembering the earth and days to follow, obtain a son, the issue of his father.

2. Thy friend loves not the friendship which considers her who is near in kindred as stranger. Sons of the mighty Asura, the Heroes, supporters of the heavens, see far around them.

3. Yea, this the Immortals seek of thee with longing,

progeny of the sole existing mortal. Then let thy soul and mine be knit together, and as a loving husband take thy consort.

4. Shall we do now what we ne'er did aforetime? We who spake righteously now talk impurely? Gandharva in the floods, the Dame of Waters—such is our bond, such our most lofty kinship.

5. Even in the womb God Tvaṣṭar, Vivifier, shaping all forms, Creator, made us consorts. None violates his holy ordinances: that we are his, heavens and earth acknowledge.

6. Who knows that earliest day whereof thou speakest? Who hath beheld it? Who can here declare it? Great is the Law of Varuṇa and Mitra. What, wanton! Wilt thou say to men to tempt them?

7. I, Yami, am possessed by love of Yama, that I may rest on the same couch beside him. I as a wife would yield me to my husband. Like car-wheels let us speed to meet each other.

8. They stand not still; they never close their eyelids, those sentinels of Gods who wander round us. Not me—go quickly, wanton, with another, and hasten like a chariot wheel to meet him.

9. May Sūrya's eye with days and nights endow him, and ever may his light spread out before him. In heaven and earth the kindred Pair commingle. On Yami be the unbrotherly act of Yama.

10. Sure there will come succeeding times when brothers and sisters will do acts unmeet for kinsfolk. Not me,

O fair one—seek another husband, and make thine arm a pillow for thy consort.

11. Is he a brother when no lord is left her? Is she a sister when Destruction cometh? Forced by my love these many words I utter. Come near, and hold me in thy close embraces.

12. I will not fold mine arms about thy body: they call it sin when one comes near his sister. Not me—prepare thy pleasures with another: thy brother seeks not this from thee, O fair one.

13. Alas! thou art indeed a weakling, Yama we find in thee no trace of heart or spirit. As round the tree the woodbine clings, another will cling about thee girt as with a girdle.

14. Embrace another, Yami; let another, even as the woodbine rings the tree, enfold thee. Win thou his heart and let him win thy fancy, and he shall form with thee a blest alliance.[30]

Thus, in the genealogy of the Sun-born, Yama and Yami, the twins, inaugurate the line that later was to become the Kuru vansh, the clan of the Kurus. The other meanings of the term Yama are 'Time' and 'Blue' or 'Dark', 'Krishna', and also 'Dharma' (not exactly 'religion', but more appropriately the 'moral law'). Yama in his supernatural aspect is related to Krishna. During the war at Kurukshetra, Krishna tells Arjuna,

---

[30]Ralph T. H. Griffith (trans.), *The Rig Veda*, 1896, 'HYMN X. Yama Yami', *Sacred Texts*, <www.sacred-texts.com/hin/rigveda/rv10010.htm> [accessed: 1 July 2021].

'Of the celestial Naga snakes I am Ananta; of the aquatic deities I am Varuja. Of departed ancestors I am Aryama and among the dispensers of law I am Yama, lord of death.'[31]

Just as in one aspect of his being Yama is present in Krishna, in another aspect, he is present in the eldest of the five Pandava brothers. Yudhishthira is born of Kunti by her desire for a son by Yama. That is the reason why Yudhishthira is called Dharmaraja. Twice in the story, Yama appears before his son. In the first instance, difficult questions are asked to Yudhishthira by Yaksha, who turns out to be none other than Yama himself. These questions address certain perennial metaphysical doubts. The second and the final time we hear of Yama in the *Mahabharata* is near the conclusion of the plot. He speaks to Yudhishthira, who has ascended to heaven and faces sambhrama (a dilemma) about the final destination of his brothers. It is then that Yama puts him to a final test and, on being satisfied with Yudhishthira's response, reveals his true form as Yama. The *Mahabharata* comes to a close here.

Of course, Yama is not the only one who is present from the beginning to the end of the *Mahabharata* story. There is also the rather mysterious Vyasa, at once a character in the story and the narrator of the story, whose claim to 'having seen it all',[32] is as viable as that of Yama. Vyasa, known as Krishna Dwaipayana, has this intriguing name connecting

---

[31]Gambhirananda (trans.), *Bhagavad Gita*, 10–29.
[32]I am alluding to the famous phrase from T. S. Eliot's classic poem 'The Love Song of J. Alfred Prufrock'.

him to Yama, since based on the claim of the Krishna of
Dwarka in the Gita, 'Krishna, in one aspect, is Yama.' Yama,
as described in the *Rig Veda*, is considered to be the Maha
Kala, the Great Arbiter of Time. Is it, therefore, possible to
read the *Mahabharata* as an epic of Time? Since Yama is not
exactly identical with death, but is the overlord of life and
death, would it be possible to understand the epic as a great
poem of Life and Death? Before we draw any inferences, let
us look into the following story:

UGRASRAVA SAUTI, the son of Lomaharshana,
a veteran storyteller, knew all of the stories that
Lomaharshana knew. On one occasion, Saunaka, most
respected by the learned people of his time, desires to
hear some of them. Suanaka says, 'In the first place, I
am desirous of hearing the history of the race of Bhrigu.
Recount thou that history, we shall attentively listen
to thee.' On Saunaka's authority, it appears that these
stories had been previously recited by Lomharshana
together with Krishna-Dwaipayana and were known
as 'Bharata'. Sauti, who knows Bharata, begins: 'The
great and blessed saint Bhrigu, we are informed, was
produced by the self-existing Brahma from the fire at
the sacrifice of Varuna. And Bhrigu had a son, named
Chyavana, whom he dearly loved. And to Chyavana was
born a virtuous son called Pramati. And Pramati had
a son named Ruru by Ghritachi (the celestial dancer).
And to Ruru also by his wife Pramadvara was born a
son, whose name was Saunaka. He was, O Saunaka, thy

great ancestor, exceedingly virtuous in his ways. He was devoted to asceticism, of great reputation, proficient in law, and eminent among those having knowledge of the Vedas.'[33]

At this point, Saunaka asks why the son of Bhrigu was named Chyavana. The history, as Sauti narrates it, is thus: Bhrigu had Puloma as his wife. A rakshasa cast an evil eye on her and manages to carry her away. As he does this, he chances upon Agni at a sacrifice place. He asks Agni, 'Since there is the fire burning in my heart for me, she is more rightfully mine and not Bhrigu's, is that not so?' Agni is in a dilemma, for it is Agni that is burning in the rakshasa's heart. He responds, 'Yes, it is true that you wanted to choose her as your wife, but it is Bhrigu who has accepted her through holy rites.'[34] The rakshasa, encouraged by this partial corroboration, takes her away. Shocked and angered by the outrage, the foetus in Puloma's womb drops down, and for this reason he obtained the name of Chyavana, meaning 'full of vitality'. The rakshasa, seeing the infant drop from the mother's womb, shining like the sun, loosens his grasp on the woman, falls down, and is instantly converted into ashes. The beautiful Puloma, distraught with grief, picks up her offspring, the son of Bhrigu, and walks away. Her tears form a great river and that river begins to follow her footsteps. And the Grandfather of the worlds, seeing the river follow the path of his son's wife, names it Vadhusara. Bhrigu is outraged by the entire

---

[33]K. M. Ganguli (trans.), 'Adi Parva, XIII', *The Mahabharata*.
[34]Ibid.

episode, and when Puloma tells him that it was Agni who had spoken to the rakshasa, he curses Agni, 'Thou shalt eat of all things.'[35]

Agni reminds him that he is the 'mouth of all gods and ancestors'—Pitrus. How could he be the unclean 'mouth that eats all'? Then Agni, after reflecting for a while, withdraws himself from all places—from places of the daily homa, the fire sacrifices, of men, all long-extending sacrifices, places of holy rites, and other ceremonies. Thereupon, the Rishis in great anxiety go to the gods and address them thus, 'Ye immaculate beings! The three regions of the universe are confounded at the cessation of their sacrifices and ceremonies in consequence of the loss of fire! Ordain what is to be done in this matter.'[36]

Then, the Rishis and the gods go together to the presence of Brahma. They tell him all about the curse on Agni and the consequent interruption of all ceremonies. The Creator of the Universe, hearing these words, summons Agni and says, 'Thou art the creator of the worlds and thou art their destroyer! Thou preserver! The three worlds and thou art the promoter of all sacrifices and ceremonies! Therefore, behave thyself so that ceremonies are not interrupted. Thou art, O fire, the supreme energy born of thy own power.' Then Agni replies to the Grandfather, 'So it be.'[37] And he then goes away to obey the command of the supreme Lord. The Gods and the Rishis

---

[35]Ibid.
[36]Ibid.
[37]Ibid.

return in delight to the place from where they had come.

Sauti said, 'Chyavana, the son of Bhrigu, begot a son in the womb of his wife Sukanya. And that son was the illustrious Pramati of resplendent energy. And Pramati begot in the womb of Ghritachi a son called Ruru. And Ruru begot on his wife Pramadvara a son called Saunaka. And I shall relate to you in detail, O Brahmana, the entire history of Ruru of abundant energy.'

Ruru and Pramadvara are the primordial lovers, ready to give life each for the other. When, Pramadvara dies of a snake bite as she is asleep in a thick green forest, the grief stricken Ruru challenges gods and asks for her to be brought back to life. His pursuit compels the messenger of gods to come to him and reveal that should he persist and should Pramadvara come back to life, he would have to give half of his life in exchange. He, the archetypal lover, agrees to the condition. 'O best of celestial messengers, I most willingly offer a moiety of my own life in favour of my bride. Then let my beloved one rise up once more in her dress and lovable form.' Then the king of Gandharvas (the father of Pramadvara) and the celestial messenger, both of excellent qualities, went to the god Dharma (the Judge of the dead) and addressed him, saying, 'If it be thy will, O Dharmaraja, let the amiable Pramadvara, the betrothed wife of Ruru, now lying dead, rise up with a moiety of Ruru's life.' And

> Dharmaraja answered, 'O messenger of the gods, if
> it be thy wish, let Pramadvara, the betrothed wife of
> Ruru, rise up endued with a moiety of Ruru's life.'[38]

What is important to note here is that Saunaka, a descendent
of the Bhrigu clan appearing at the beginning of the *Adi
Parva*, sets the narrative of the *Mahabharata* going. The epic,
also known in Indian tradition as itihasa, is thus a way of
remembering. It may be possible to say that it is a poetic
triumph that weaves together the mythological memory of
the Vedic civilization beginning with mythic persons such
as Yama and Yami, riding on chariots, as well as the line of
succession of clans, mainly the Ruru clan. It is a synoptic
reflection of how the social order moved from that of the
pastoral Vedic people to that of feudal kingdoms ruled by a
warrior class. As the account of the war makes it abundantly
clear, it is a large-frame picture of the creation of an empire.
Sri Aurobindo, commenting on the epic, points out that it
would be a misreading of the poem if one overlooks the
alignment of kings and princes from across India who had
joined the two factions of the Kurus, not out of personal
affiliations but because of political realism:

> The preceding events are therefore of essential
> importance to the epic. 'Without the war, no
> *Mahabharata*,' is true of this epic; but without the
> causes of the war, no war, is equally true. And it must
> be remembered that the Hindu narrative poets had

---

[38]Ibid.

no artistic predilections like that of the Greeks for beginning a story in the middle. On the contrary, they always preferred to begin at the beginning.

We therefore naturally expect to find the preceding political conditions and the immediate causes of the war related in the earlier part of the epic and this is precisely what we do find.... Like the continent of Europe, the ancient continent of India was subject to two opposing forces, one centripetal which was continually causing attempts at universal empire, another centrifugal which was continually impelling the empires once formed to break up again into their constituent parts: but both these forces were much stronger in the action than they have been in Europe.[39]

Sri Aurobindo presents at length the relations and tensions between the kingdoms such as Kosala, Magadha, Videha, Panchala, Bhoja, and many small rulers in the South. He adds that prior to the Kurukshetra war, five attempts were made towards empire building, four by the rulers of the Ikshavku clan and the fifth by Bharata of the Kuru clan. The alignment of the kings during the war at Kurukshetra had much to do with the political history of India during the later Vedic times.[40] Hence, though not directly related to the life and struggles of the grandchildren of Shantanu,[41] the love

---

[39]Aurobindo, *The Mahabharata*, p. 18.

[40]Ibid., p. 19.

[41]Shantanu is the king of Hastinapur, begetter of eight children from Ganga, one of whom is Bhishma, and two from his second wife Satyavati—

story of Ruru and Pramadvara becomes important for the *Mahabharata* plot. Essentially a love story, like the Greek myth of Orpheus and Eurydice, it has inspired Indian poets in many different literary periods. One of the most beautiful renderings of this episode is in Sri Aurobindo's long poem, composed in English towards the end of the nineteenth century under the title *Love and Death*.

Just as empire building and the resultant political tussles arising out of that ambition are concerns explored in the *Mahabharata*, reconstructing the past of the clan over the preceding several centuries and reconnecting with memories of the mythical past have been subject matters of the epic, drawing upon the normative constants of the moral order and dwelling deep into human emotions. Similarly, love and death have been among the central elements in the thematic web of the *Mahabharata*. This brings us to briefly look at one of the most fascinating characters in the whole of world literature: Kunti, the wife of Pandu and the mother of the Pandavas. It would not be any exaggeration to say that in terms of fullness and complexity of delineation, there hardly is a match for her in any other epic, play, or novel in any language. From the very beginning, her life is a strange mix of the extraordinary and the tragic. The narrative of her life begins in the sixty-first canto of the *Sambhava Parva*, which forms a part of the *Adi Parva*: 'There was amongst the Yadavas a chief named Sura. He was the father of Vasudeva. And he had a daughter

---

Chitravirya and Vichitravirya. He is the Grandfather of the Kauravas and the Pandavas.

called Pritha, who was unrivalled for beauty on earth.'[42] She is given a boon by a sage which empowers her to invoke and summon any god for having children by them. This made Pritha—later known by the name Kunti—curious. As soon as she recited the Mantra and invoked Vivaswata, the Sun-god, he approached her and asked for her bidding. When she revealed her intention, Vivaswata gratified her and of their union was born Karna, the eldest son of Pritha. But, as she was not yet married, she feared the censure that might come due to her transgression and decided to leave the luminous child in the river waters. Later, having been chosen to marry Pandu, the king of Hastinapur, she married him and as Kunti, Pandu's wife, gave birth to three more sons—Yudhishthira, Bhima, and Arjuna, each time invoking a different god.

Karna, her first son continued to grow in the household of a Suta, a family not from the Kshatriya class or clan and came to be regarded as a Suta-putra, a person not at par in social standing with Kunti's other three children, the princes growing up in Hastinapur.

It is Kunti, her abandoned child Karna, and her nephew Krishna who together occupy most pervasively the heart of the *Mahabharata* story.

THE BEGINNING AND THE END
Before one explores the importance of the thematically crucial characters in the plot, it would be necessary to state that up until this point in the story, up to the Ruru–Pramadvara

---

[42]K. M. Ganguli (trans.), 'Adi Parva', CXI, *The Mahabharata*.

episode, the narrator Sauti has invoked most of the major Vedic deities: Indra, Yama, Agni, Varuna, and Surya. It may be in order to briefly remind ourselves the place of these gods in the Vedic symbolism and world view. As is known among scholars dealing with the history of civilization, the genesis of most deities in the Egyptian, Greek, Syrian, and Vedic accounts needs to be seen primarily in relation to natural phenomena—the vast expanse of the sky, light and darkness, and fire and water. Vivasvan, imagined male and meaning 'light', and Saranya, imagined female and meaning 'dawn', are the parents of the Ashwins, who are conceptualized as being twins. The Ashwins are a very important component of the *Rig Veda*, mentioned 376 times.[43] They are present in the beginning of the *Mahabharata* story in the *Adi Parva*. They are also an important part of the story of the epic since it is from them that two of the Pandava siblings, Nakula and Sahadeva—always to be spoken as being together—are born. In their form, the Ashwins enter the epic. Likewise, Varuna, in his form as Vayu, enters the epic plot in the form of Bhima. Surya, in the form of Karna, and Indra, in the form of Arjuna, enhance the link between the *Mahabharata* story and the pantheon of an earlier age. There is also Yama, the begetter of Yudhishthira, who brings fullness to the rainbow bridge between the world of the gods as imagined by the early Vedic civilization and the era of the *Mahabharata*. Kunti is the main vehicle of this continuity. So is Krishna, perhaps; but

---

[43]'Ashwins', *Vyasa Mahabharata*, <www.vyasaonline.com/encyclopedia/ashwins> [accessed 12 June 2020].

probably, he symbolizes change more than continuity. I shall take up this point later in the book.

Kunti, also named Pritha, as the *Mahabharata* story goes, is the daughter of Shurasena and adopted by the king Kuntibhoja. Pritha has a brother, Vasudeva, who is the father of Krishna. Shurasena had given away Kunti to his childless cousin, Kuntibhoja, to adopt. All of them belong to the Yadava clan, who are a pastoral people, tending cows and multiplying the herds being their main interest. They would not have been intertwined with the Bhrigus, a warring Kshatriya clan, had it not been for the accident of marriage between Kunti and Pandu. The epic depicts Kunti as an exceedingly beautiful and graceful woman with manners that could please her family, kings, heroes, and rishis alike. On one occasion, when Durvasa, a rishi difficult to manage and known for his anger, was on a visit to Kuntibhoja, he was so pleased with her graceful devotion that he gave her a very unusual boon. After he left, in order to test the power of the boon, she invoked Surya, and had Karna as her firstborn son. She abandoned this child, as Paris was abandoned by his parents in Homer's *Iliad*. Later, she was married to Pandu. If Kunti had received a boon, Pandu had received a curse. The curse was a result of Pandu wrongfully shooting an arrow at Rishi Kindama and his wife as they were mating in the form of deer. The curse foretold that if Pandu ever attempted to make love, he too would instantly die. In order to avoid that fate, he asks Kunti to use her boon. She does so three times and gives birth to Yudhishthira, Bhima, and Arjuna. Since Pandu had taken one more wife, Madri, who too yearns to have children, Pandu asks Kunti to use the same method for her too. Madri thus gives birth to Nakula and Sahadeva, born of the Ashwins. Thus, the gods, as gods were imagined in the early Vedic civilization, are brought into the plot of the epic. Meanwhile, the clan of Kuru has continued, taking difficulties and triumphs in its stride as it reaches to the generation of Pandu and Dhritarashtra. The story of continuation of the clan is exceedingly gripping despite the plenitude of its members across several generations. Just as Kunti and Krishna are the key characters in the story on the Yadava side, Bhishma is the key character in the Kuru clan. I offer here a simple outline of the clan for easy reference.

A good starting point for following the plot of the *Mahabharata* epic is to begin with the reign of Shantanu, two generations after Bharata, the semi-mythical hero after whom the poem gets its title. Shantanu was first married to Ganga, and after Ganga returned to her otherworldly abode, to Satyavati. Shantanu and Ganga gave birth to eight children, seven of whom Ganga deliberately offered to the river Ganga. Only one, the last-born Devarata, was saved by Shantanu before she made the offering. The *Mahabharata* is silent about Ganga after this. Shantanu married Satyavati after several years, by when Devarata had fully grown up. On Satyavati's father's insistence, Devarata took an oath to remain unmarried so that Shantanu was succeeded by one of her sons. Satyavati had two sons, Chitravirya (also known as Chitrangada) and Vichitravirya. Bhishma kidnaps three princesses of the Kashi kingdom. He gets two of them, Ambika and Ambalika, married to Vichitravirya. They give birth to one son each, not born of Vichitravirya but of Vyasa. Vyasa's appearance terrifies the two women—during the act of copulation, one completely closes her eyes, while the other goes pale with fear. Due to these circumstances of the forced continuation of the Kuru line, the son of Ambika is born blind and named Dhritarashtra. The son of Ambalika is Pandu, who is born completely pale, and is so named after the Sanskrit word for the colour. The blind Dhritarashtra is married to Gandhari, who emulates her husband and blindfolds herself for the rest of her life. Gandhari is the sister of Shakuni, who, later in the story, plays the role of the wicked advisor to the Kaurava princes. Pandu first marries Kunti and later Madri. However, both Pandu and Madri die before the war begins.

Dhritarashtra and Gandhari have numerous children—a girl named Duhsala, and ninety-eight boys, including Duryodhana and Dushasana. Barring Karna, whom Kunti had abandoned before her marriage, her three sons and the two of Madri are the five Pandavas. All the five Pandava brothers take Draupadi as their shared wife on the instruction of their mother. Arjuna has another wife, the sister of Krishna, Subhadra. Arjuna and Subhadra give birth to Abhimanyu, who is later married to Uttara. Before Abhimanyu's death in the war at a tender age, Uttara conceives and later gives birth to Parikshita. Married to Madravati, Parikshita has a son called Janamejaya. If one were to make sense of this maze of characters, each one of them more heroic than the other, and try to think of a single line of lineage leaving out the branches where the Kuru clan line comes to an end, it would read: Shantanu, Vichitravirya, Pandu, Arjuna, Abhimanyu,

Parikshita, and Janamejaya. Of these seven generations, three are directly involved in the war, two precede it and the remaining two are the generations that follow the war. However, in the epic, the last two generations are mentioned in the very first book, the *Adi Parva*, creating an impression that Parikshita and Janamejaya and the snake-sacrifice ritual, the sarpa yagnya, precede the war. The arrangement is possible as the *Mahabharata* was composed *after* the war. That, however, cannot be evidence enough to confirm the historical accuracy of the poem as a history of the great war described in the *Mahabharata*.

It is possible in a poem, particularly in an epic, to begin the narrative not at the temporal beginning of the plot but at the end or the middle of the story. Most Western epics are expected to begin in medias res, somewhere in the middle of the story. Thus, Janamejaya and Parikshita appearing at the beginning of the poem can be seen as a technique employed towards emphasizing the historical 'authenticity' of what is to follow in the poem as the account of a great transition, the end of an epoch, Yuganta, and the beginning of a new one. Of the members of the Kuru clan, the ones who participate in the war are Bhishma; the Kauravas Duryodhana, Dushasana, and their ninety-eight brothers; the four children of Kunti, that is Karna and the first three Pandavas; the two children of Madri; and Abhimanyu. Of them, all but Yudhishthira, Arjuna, Bhima, Nakula, and Sahadeva are killed in the Great War. There are many other kings and princes involved as well. Their armies get entirely destroyed. There are teachers of the Kuru princes, who too get killed. After the war, the elder generation—Kunti, Gandhari, Dhritarashtra, and Vidura—move to dwell in a forest. All of them die in a forest fire. Krishna, who joins the war as Arjuna's charioteer, dies in his own country—some sixty-eight years later—in a state of anarchy that his Yadava clan has created in the kingdom. After Krishna's death, the five Pandavas and their wife, together with a dog, start walking north towards the mountains and they drop dead one by one on the way, except Yudhishthira, or Dharmaraja. Of course, they are reunited in the other world. There, the story of the war and the ascension to Svarga come to an end.

2

THE WHEEL

MYTH AND DHARMA

In most epics, the supernatural plays a role in bringing the
epic action to a successful conclusion. In the *Mahabharata*,
the supernatural is used for creating symmetry of power, a
balance of strength, and an endless action in which every
seeming end is emptied of glory. The first generation in the
poem, the generation of Shantanu, comes face to face with
the supernatural when Ganga appears on the scene. And, as
with every character and every event in the epic, there is a
story behind this. A powerful king from the Ikshvaku dynasty
whose name was Mahabhisha had been to Brahma's court,
where Ganga was present. When a chance breeze blew at
her clothes, he kept staring at her revealed limbs. He did this
when everyone else had bent their heads out of politeness.
Ganga too enjoyed his gaze. But Brahma was angry with both
of them. In order to atone for her misdemeanour, she was
asked to go to Manushya loka, the human realm. Later, on one
occasion the Kuru king Pratipa was in meditation. Ganga saw
him and sat on his right thigh. The general custom was that
the right thigh was for daughters to sit, the left thigh for wives.
She asked him if he would take her in marriage but Pratipa

offered to have her as his daughter-in-law instead and asked her to marry his son, Shantanu. She agreed to do so. This would be her atonement for her behaviour in Brahma's court. Having married Shantanu on the condition that he would not question any of her actions, she manages to 'release' the first seven of the children born to her. Difficulty arises though when the eighth child is born. This son is initially named Devarata but is known through the rest of the poem and through his long life as Bhishma.

In the battlefield, Bhishma's war skills, wisdom, and acumen are pitted against the wisdom and vision of Krishna. Quite strikingly, Krishna too is the eighth child born to his mother, Devaki. The first six of her children are killed by her brother, Kamsa, in order to protect himself from a prophecy that her eighth child would bring his downfall. The seventh child, Balarama, is saved, but has to grow up in isolation. Krishna, the avenger of Kamsa, is the eighth child. It is evident from the very early years of his life that he possesses supernatural powers. Both Bhishma and Krishna are shown in the poem as fighting the war not for themselves but for the opposing sides of warriors, the Kauravas and Pandavas. Yet, they control the progress of the combat. Both live to the very end of the war, and both are completely dismayed at the destruction it causes.

Towards the end of the war, on the eighteenth day, the last major combat takes place between Duryodhana and Bhima. Duryodhana has offered Bhima the choice of the weapon to be used in combat, and Bhima has chosen the gada yuddh, or combat using mace. Krishna knows that Duryodhana is specially blessed by his mother, Gandhari, and his body, like that of Achilles in Homer's epic, is invincible. However, there is a catch. When Duryodhana had received the blessing from his mother, he was almost entirely unclad, barring the leaves which served as his loincloth. And it is that area, which had not received the 'protective energy' passed on to him by Gandhari, which has remained vulnerable. In a gada yuddh, the conventions of war had set that a warrior would not strike the adversary below the navel. Since Krishna knows about the secret blessing received by Duryodhana, he persuades Bhima to violate this rule and strike Duryodhana on his thighs, smashing them and eventually leading to his death. Duryodhana was trained in the gada yuddh by Balarama, Krishna's elder brother. Balarama, therefore, takes avenging the killing of Duryodhana as his personal responsibility. The war that should have ended at this point continues.

The next combat takes place between Ashwathama and Arjuna, somewhere close to Vyasa's ashram. Assessing the might of the arm of the adversary, they decide to use the bramhastra, a special arm gifted to both of them by the gods themselves. Seeing the destruction entailed in the use of these arms, Vyasa asks them to withdraw the astras. Arjuna knew how to do this. But Ashwathama knew only how to launch it but not how to reverse its course. He therefore directs it at Uttara to kill Abhimanyu's child growing within her. This angers Vyasa and he asks Ashwathama to give the lustrous diamond that is part of his forehead to Krishna, creating a deep wound that would never heal and would continue to bleed forever. Ashwathama is one of the seven mythological immortals. He turns away to the forest to wander forever, carrying his unhealing wound with him. The war thus comes to an end. There are many other examples of the supernatural or the mythic playing a decisive role in advancing the plot of the *Mahabharata*.

When we encounter myths, the usual questions about the probability or possibility of the events occurring in it are kept completely out of consideration, exercising what the poet Coleridge described as 'a willing suspension of disbelief'.[44] In the mythic world, gods, goddesses, ghosts, demons, and spirits can be in conversation with humans, animals, plants, fish, and birds. That world has a trans-species view of existence which knows neither the limits of time nor space. However, myths are no hallucination, nor are they an expression of fantasy. While hallucination and fantasy are peculiar to a single individual at the time of their occurrence, myths are a kind of truth which the entire community accepts as a 'given'; and this acceptance can stay unchallenged for centuries. They are, it would be fair to argue, a collective dream of an entire civilization.

At the turn of the nineteenth century, Europe witnessed a sudden spurt in books documenting myths from different parts of the world, which in turn created a scientific interest in them. This resulted in the works of Sigmund Freud and

---

[44]Expression made immortal by the British Romantic poet S. T. Coleridge, who used it to describe how poetry is not expected to be realistic and how readers can construct alternate realities as guided by the aesthetic framework of a literary text. See 'Chapter XIV', *Biographia Literaria*, 1817, <https://web.english.upenn.edu/~mgamer/Etexts/biographia.html>.

Karl Jung. In their analyses, myths were representations of collective desires, anxieties, and fears. Freud, in fact, used some of the Greek mythical figures to explain his theory of relations dominated by incest and sexual obsessions. His discussion of the Electra complex and the Oedipus complex uses the mythical to establish psycho-medical conclusions. Jung went a step further and introduced the concept of archetypes, representation of human attributes or desires in the form of mythic characters, and plot elements. The *Mahabharata* generously deploys the use of myth. A number of characters are cursed, and some are blessed. In many cases, a blessing or a curse leads to the plot progressing. Pandu, Krishna, Karna, and Arjuna have to face curses; Bhishma, Savitri, Kunti, and Sanjaya have earned special boons. Divine acts such as Krishna intervening during Draupadi's disrobing or Jayadratha's killing,[45] too, help to move the plot forward. Gods, Gandharvas, Rakshas, Daityas—the denizens of Patala, the Underworld—frequent Manushya loka. The realm of human beings and heroes also visit Indra loka, the realm of immortal beings.

Though I am not aware if any social scientist has analysed the operation of myth in the *Mahabharata*, it may indeed be possible to employ Freud and Jung's theories to study this. That may, to some extent, throw light on the psychological transactions of individuals for whom the *Mahabharata* myths

---

[45]Jayadratha, was the husband of Duhsala, the only sister of the Kauravas, and the sovereign of the Sindhu kingdom. In a lewd gesture, he had exposed himself to Draupadi as she was being disrobed.

are 'real'. However, the method may not be similarly useful in understanding the epic itself. Therefore, I would like to propose here that it would be useful to consider if the mythic world that breathes life into the story of the *Mahabharata* story has any purpose, and why the makers of the epic felt the need to use myths at crucial junctures of the story.

It is important to state here that the *Mahabharata* does not *employ* myth as a literary element, it *produces* myth, and is entirely an extended myth by itself. This is not to say that the war in the *Mahabharata* is entirely a fantasy, fiction, or the product of pure imagination. It no doubt is itihas, a manner of remembering the events in the past, but in order to imbue the retelling of that history with dignity and grandeur, the narrative is painted as if all of the events that occur in it belong to a timeless and ever-present era. In order to achieve this effect, practically every character and every major event in the poem has been given a generous touch of the unusual, and they do not operate within the reality of human space and human time. Thus, Shakuntala, the mother of Bharata, is shown as born of a celestial and deathless apsara, and Dushyanta, her lover and a mortal king, is shown as being able to frequent Indra loka. Shantanu, too, is shown in the realm of deathless beings when he first sees his future consort. Ganga herself is able to return to the world of Indra at will. Her human child spends his initial years with her, in the world of the celestial beings, gaining all the knowledge that humans so far possessed. Kunti in the next generation is born because of a blessing, and all of her four sons are fathered by gods. Pandu dies of a curse while attempting to copulate with Madri. Madri has children because Kunti invokes the twin Ashwins. Dhritarashtra is shown most unrealistically as someone who sires a hundred sons and a daughter, something possible in myths alone. Krishna is more a mythical person rather than a human hero, and is shown to possess the power of working miracles. Bhishma can extend the moment of his death by several days or months, till the sun enters the northern hemisphere of the Earth, as he keeps lying on a bed of arrows, the sharshaiya. Karna is born from Surya and receives both special blessings and fatal curses. Abhimanyu is able to learn a difficult war strategy while still in the womb of his mother. Draupadi can invoke Krishna when she is in distress, and he provides her never-ending vesture when the Kaurvas attempt her disrobing.

One can go on recounting how in numerous ways each of the characters depicted in the epic are quite consciously removed from natural time and space, how each one of them live and act as if they are part of another order of existence, as if they are characters within a myth rather than actors in history. In Homer's epics, the increasing disconnect between the ancient Greek myths and the history of the region around the Aegean Sea is the focus of concern. In Vyasa's epic, it is presenting the political history of the subcontinent as if it belongs to mythical times. One of the reasons for the continuity of the *Mahabharata* and its mesmerizing appeal is its ability to use history to enliven myth, not its use of myth to substantiate history. In all historical ages following the *Mahabharata*, the myths that Indians have been drawn to are primarily from the *Mahabharata*, and also from the

Ramayana. They should have come from the *Rig Veda*, it being historically much older than the *Mahabharata* and the *Ramayana*. They could have come from the numerous Puranas too, which were written in later centuries, since the express purpose of the Puranas was to consciously sound, and be, mythical. Still, there is a certain lack of credibility that the Puranas suffer from as 'believable' narratives. The audiences of the Puranas know in their hearts, and they knew this in all ages, that the narrative to be encountered there is incredible, intentionally designed to be a hyperbole. The *Mahabharata* does not suffer from the same charge. Despite its use of the mythic mode in drawing up its characters and episodes, it is seen as being a kind of history, albeit about a time long, long ago.

The widespread misconception that the *Mahabharata* war took place some 5,000 years ago, that the epic was composed some 4,000 years or so before our time, arises out of its unique method of mythologizing history, a method which none could employ as convincingly as Vyasa. Centuries after the epic was written, no one has been able to vie with him, let alone surpass him. In one of the episodes, when Arjuna wanted to kill Drona but could not have managed it without recourse to strategy, Krishna gets an elephant with the same name as Drona's son, Ashwathama, killed, and spreads the word to distract the valiant Dronacharya. When Drona asks if Ashwathama was dead, Yudhishthira, known for always speaking the truth, is prompted by Krishna to respond, 'naro va kunjaro va', 'Yes, but I am not sure if man or elephant'. This has its desired effect and the Pandavas finally achieve their goal in battle for the day. When one tries to decide if Vyasa's *Mahabharata* is myth or history, the judgement can only be 'Yes, eminently, history or myth'; so organically are the two welded. It would be futile to claim it either way, for it is both, because it is at once both.

Myth apparently has a plot, but the plot does not have to be governed by the laws of probability. This being so, new layers can be added to it by others who share the framework of the narrative. That is how the *Mahabharata* could be told and retold in different ways over the centuries and new material could be added to it without causing much unease to the original. The story of Shantanu meeting Ganga is told in the 'critical edition' and in most *Mahabharata* traditions one way, but it can also be narrated differently, as the following passage from a Rajasthani *Mahabharata* does:

> There is a frog. It decides to go to the Ganga River. On the way, it gets maimed by wandering cattle. Its soul enters the body of a baby about to be born in the family of a small-time trader. On becoming an adult, the baby boy starts disliking the family profession. So, he decides to go to Indra. Now Indra looks at this boy and feels very amused that such a boy who knows next to nothing has such an ambition. So, Indra sarcastically tells him that he would employ this boy as his advisor. The offer is promptly accepted. But Indra fails to pay to the boy all the big salary he had agreed to pay. On a morning when the boy is sitting outside his house doing *datun*, brushing his teeth with twig of a tree, he spots

a woman who is cleaning the streets. And he is smitten by her. He approaches her...but he only says 'You are my sister. What can I give to you?' She says, 'Normally I don't get good clothes. If you give me some clothes, I'll be happy.' So, he decides to give her clothes stolen from Indrani's robes made of gold. A few days later this woman goes to Indra's city, the Indraprasth. Indra sees her and gets very wild. 'Only the Indrani can use such clothes, how can this woman use such clothes? Who is the idiot who has given her such clothes?' So, the boy is accused. The *Indra-sabha* is convened. 'You must immediately be sacked because only Indrani can wear such clothes,' commands Indra. So, this boy is sacked. But he says, 'Wait, you're sacking me but you never paid my wages, so give all those wages to me.' Indra says, 'But I never kept any account.' It was indeed a huge amount. Indra ends up giving him several maunds of coins. The boy says, 'Of course, I have to go back home but before that why don't I go and visit Ganga once.' So, he fares forth to Ganga and on the way, one of the bullocks of the cart in which he is travelling collapses. It is already dark. There is forest on all sides. So this boy prays to Surya. Surya appears and demands, 'I can rescue you provided you give me some bribe.' Half of the coins go to Surya. Immediately, the bullock comes back to life and the young boy, rather the young man, reaches the Ganga River. Struck by her beauty, he says, 'What will I do with all the wealth that I have, I'm going to give half of my wealth to Ganga.' So he sinks half of the money into the river. Then on his way back Surya stops him and says, 'Where is my half?' He says, 'but I gave your half to Ganga, my half is with me.' *Suryadeva* says, 'this is unfair, this is not how a self-respecting tribal ever behaves. You are behaving like a wolf, you'll become a wolf.' So the young man instantly turned into a wolf.

He is angry, and he starts chasing Ganga, as he had suffered because of Ganga. Ganga starts running, goes to her *guru*, her *guru* protects her for a while but not for a very long time. And finally—after many strange things happen to both of them—Ganga decides to marry the man turned into a wolf. It is at the moment of their wedding that the wolf returns to a human form; and it is revealed in the story for the first time that his name is Shantanu.[46]

When the framework of a story is mythic, numberless narrative possibilities open up. The question, however, is why a poet of Vyasa's phenomenal poetic power would want to take recourse to myth when he could have simply written a great historical narrative. His use of myth was so 'natural' and spellbinding that rarely in the past have critics and commentators in India questioned his need to frame the historical narrative by completely submerging it in myth. However, it is nearly impossible to begin understanding what the epic is about unless we ask this question. Having asked it, in however crude a manner, I would like to propose

---

[46]Bhagwandas Patel, 'The Bhil Mahabharata', G. N. Devy (ed.), *Painted Words: An Anthology of Tribal Literature*, New Delhi: Penguin Books, 2003.

that the *Mahabharata* epic, as composed by the poet of its original oral version establishes a method or a perspective of structuring historical narratives. Not only is history—or what he considered to be history—the main subject of the narrative, but the method of looking at history is also, perhaps more importantly so, the aim of the poem. That was the history of a great transition of a civilization from the early Vedic period to the period when kingship had become an accepted norm and the subcontinent had begun to be dominated by various dynasties. The entire transition was spread over a substantially long period of nearly half a millennium. To weave together the sensibilities of two strikingly different cultural periods would be a tremendous challenge for any poet. The poet who composed *Bharata*, therefore, chose to bring together the mythic past and the historical past into a single narrative, without treating one as being superior to the other. The past for the original poet of the *Bharata* was as much the past in time as it was the recollection of the past in the mind. The seamless combining of the two was also his comment on the course of the history of Indian civilization till the time of the Kurukshetra war: it was history whose distinctive features were assimilation, synthesis, combination, acceptance, and moving forward without exclusions.

The success that the *Bharata* achieved in combining myth and history is what potentially made it one of the foremost epics shaping the historical memory of India. In evolving his unique method of historical representation, the original poet of the epic also defined for centuries to come the essential nature of holding together multiple memory traditions; and that was a grand statement of acceptance, synthesis, and inclusion. That is also the reason why, while many other religious works, such as the Shastras which proposed varna-difference, led to the consolidation of social orthodoxies, the *Mahabharata* continued to be used, rendered, and re-rendered by the non-Brahminical classes, continued to be loved and adored by them, and it still inspires subsequent generations. When the later poet who brought together the many narratives in oral existence under the rubric of the *Mahabharata*, India had already gone through a fierce conflict between Vedic thought, rituals, and social and political structures and Buddhist ideas, practices, views, and political consolidation. The larger *Bharata*, the *Mahabharata,* chose primarily to remain away from these contemporary debates and stuck to the epic's vision of Bharat, a poem of a grand synthesis.

Historically, the rise and influence of Buddhism from the time of the Buddha till the time of the reorganised *Mahabharata* by Vyasa is already well established. The history of the conflict between Buddhism and the Vedic view of the world is also well known. Therefore, one cannot overlook the possibility of the *Mahabharata* having imbibed some key Buddhist symbols and integrated them into the narrative. This brings in the question of dhamma and an even larger question of chakra. Both need to be viewed in perspective in order to not misconstrue the purpose of the epic, the original as well as its larger version. In popular imagination, the central role of Sri Krishna in the original poem and the subsequent addition of the *Bhagavad Gita* have created an impression that the *Mahabharata* is a dharma grantha. Besides Yudhishthira's other name, Dharmaraja, that has helped in enhancing this belief, two verses from the *Gita*, which as a result of being oft-quoted are extremely popular, have contributed to this impression. The particular shlokas are Chapter 3, shloka 35: *shreyan svadharmo vigunah, pardharmat svanushthitat; svadharme nidhanam shreyah, paradharmo bhayavahah*, which reads in translation, 'one's own duty, though defective, is superior to another's duty well-performed. Death is better while engaged in one's own duty; another's duty is fraught with fear;'[47] and Chapter 4, shloka 7, which reads: '*yada yada hi dharmasya glanirbhavati Bharat, abhyutthanam dharmasya tadatman srujamyaham,*' or 'O scion of the Bharata dynasty, whenever there is a decline of virtue and increase of vice, and then do I manifest myself.'[48] The immense popularity of these verses need not make us impervious to the fact that neither the original *Bharata,* nor the compendious *Mahabharata* compiled centuries later had in them these verses. And, in any case, the meaning of the term 'dharma' would be significantly different for the earliest reciters of the *Bharata*. For the ancestors of the society that would have first listened to the *Bharata*, the term, arising out of the root 'dhru' or 'dhri'—with the vocalic 'r'—would have meant 'order' or 'the natural order', 'an invisible principle holding life together' or 'the holder of Time'. They would

---

[47]Gambhirananda (trans.), *Bhagavad Gita*, p. 166.
[48]Ibid., p. 180.

not have understood a dharma with deities, with a creation story and a set of prescriptions for the spiritual conduct of humans. That understanding emerged in India much later.

A set of texts produced between 3–5 centuries BCE came to be known as the *Dharmasutras*. Prior to them, the Vedas and the Upanishads continued to use the term 'dharma' primarily in its Vedic sense mentioned above. There appears to be a reason for the compilation of the *Dharmasutra* texts. Twenty-six centuries before our time, and a couple of centuries before the first *Dharmasutra* was compiled by Apastamba, a set of Sutras were compiled in the Pali language by the followers of Gautama Buddha. The most well-known among the authors of the *Dharmasutras* are Apastamba, Gautama, Baudhayana, and Vasishta. The names Gautama and Baudhayana need not be confused with either the historical person Gautama Buddha or any of the texts arising out of his teachings. I shall comment on the Buddhist text a little later, but at this stage it would be necessary to mention that the emergence of the *Dharmasutra* texts in Sanskrit would best be understood as a response to the non-Vedic stream of thought that had been spreading in all parts of India. The tussle between Buddhism and Vedic thought continued in India nearly for a thousand years since the Buddha's times. Probably, the theatre of this 'dharmic clash' extended deep into the South as well. During the fourth century, the great Tamil poet Thiruvalluvar produced a momentous text which is remembered as the *Thirukkural*. This kural was substantially similar in content and intent to the *Dharmasutras* produced in Sanskrit six or seven centuries before his time.

The *Dharmasutras* have been translated into English several times and a rich tradition of commentary on them exists. In 1879, George Buhler brought out translations of the Sutras by Apastamba and Gautama. A few years later, he published the Sutras of Baudhayana and Vasishtha. These texts were primarily interested in laying down the norms of individual and social behaviour of Brahmins. Since then, there has been a significant amount of analytical scholarship on them. One of the recent works is Patrick Olivelle's *Dharmasutras: The Law Codes of Ancient India*, which contains translations of the four major Sutra-texts as well as a critical commentary. Speaking about the typical structure of these texts, Olivelle comments:

> All the *Dharmasutras* begin with an examination of the sources of *dharma*, and this practice is followed even in the later *Smrtis*. Thereafter, the structure is not uniform. Apastamba has the most straightforward structure: initiation and the duties of a student; return home and the duties of such a young adult, followed by a parenthetical section on the initiation rituals; marriage and the duties of household life; and finally the king and the administration of justice. He deals with procreation and family continuity, inheritance, adoption, and the like within the obligations of a householder. Penances, on the other hand, are included within the discussion of the young adult who has completed his studies. This probably reflects the early structure of Dharma texts.[49]

---

[49]Patrick Olivelle (trans.), *Dharmasutras: The Law Codes of Ancient India,*

The prescriptions listed in the Sutras arise out of the *Samaveda* and the *Yajurveda* which were meant for the community that consolidated itself in the post-Vedic period as Brahmins. The *Dharmasutras*, which were being produced copiously during the three centuries preceding the Common Era (3–1 CE) and laid down the norms of action and thought in relation to social, ethical, and liturgical affairs, culminated in a text like the *Manusmriti*, which codified these norms in a kind of social-legislative framework. The *Manusmruti* took this task of codification to a point where the idea of varna became the bedrock of social ethics, inter-varna relations, and the individual's responsibilities and obligations towards maintaining and perpetuating the varna hierarchy. There is little of value in these texts for the spiritual affairs of individuals or the larger Indian society. It is well established that the larger text of the *Mahabharata* was brought together around the same historical period as the *Dharmasutras*. However, there does not appear to be any explicit mutual influence or relation between the epic and the Sutras of the Vedic Brahmin scholars. In fact, despite the presence of the *Bharata* in the earlier oral tradition, the line of kings and ancestors mentioned in the *Dharmasutras* is entirely at divergence. Therefore, the dharma of the ancient Brahminical *Dharmasutras* and the dharma articulated in the *Mahabharata* do not have much in common except for the language in which they were written. The fact that these were texts in Sanskrit and written around roughly the same

New Delhi: Oxford University Press, 1999.

time need not be taken as justification for the claim that the *Mahabharata* is a text about dharma as understood in the *Dharmasutras*.

The term 'dharma' in Sanskrit has its equivalent 'dhamma' in ancient Pali usage, the language in which the discourses of Gautama Buddha were first recorded. He used the term to describe the mental qualities of an individual progressing towards nirvana. His teachings are preserved in the texts known as 'pitaka', meaning basket or container, there being three major pitakas: *Sutrapitaka*, *Vinayapitaka*, and *Abhidamaapitaka*. The first of these three contains Buddha's canon, known as the *Dhammapada*, or the path of Dharma. It comprises over 400 precepts distributed into 26 sections. This text lays down the successive stages in the spiritual journey of a person, ultimately bringing one to the realization of the 'deathless ground of life'. What it lays down is in sharp contrast to the *Dharmasutras* which rose out of the Brahminical tradition a few centuries later.

As the Buddha states,

It is not the matted hair nor birth that makes a Brahmin, but truth and the love for all of life with which one's heart is full. What use is matted hair? What use is a deerskin on which to sit for meditation, if your mind still seethes with lust? Saffron robe and outward show do not make a Brahmin, but training of the mind and senses through practice of meditation. Neither riches nor high caste make a Brahmin. Free yourself from selfish desires, and you will become a Brahmin. He has

83

thrown off his chains; he trembles not in fear. No selfish
bonds can ensnare him, no impure thought pollute his
mind. That one I call a Brahmin who has cut through
the strap and thong and chain of karma. He has got up
from sleep, fully awake. Him I call Brahmin who fears
neither prison nor death. He has the power of love no
army can defeat.[50]

Needless to say, the kind of moral order that the *Bharata*
prescribed was very different from the moral responsibility
that the Buddha speaks about. It would, therefore, be
judicious to maintain that the epic narrative *Bharata* and
the *Dhammapada* of The Enlightened had not crossed paths.
It would also be justified to add that the dharma at the heart
of the *Mahabharata* was concerned with the origins and
development of a people who had been on the move for a
long time and had at one point in time decided to settle down
and form kingdoms. It is, in a way, the dharma iconically
symbolized by the chakra.

It has been a convention to depict on the cover page of
the *Bhagavad Gita* the image of Arjuna on a chariot with Sri
Krishna as the charioteer. This practice is so well-established
that the printed *Gita* may appear almost incomplete without
the visual preface. Krishna as seen in this image has one
arm twined with the reins of the horses storming into the
battlefield. The other arm is shown as slightly raised towards
the skies, with one of his fingers supporting a lustrous disk,

---

[50]Eknath Eswaran (trans.), *The Dhammapada,* New Delhi: Penguin Books,
1986, pp. 196–97.

the chakra. Krishna's chakra is described in ancient Indian mythology as the Sudarshan Chakra, the ultimate weapon with an unmatched divine power which has been gifted to Krishna alone. The chakra originally was associated with the 'su-darshan'—delightful to view—Vishnu. Later, as Krishna came to be seen as the human manifestation of Vishnu, his association with the chakra grew in importance. The *Rig Veda* describes Vishnu in its Mandala 164, hymns 6–14. A somewhat awkward English translation renders the hymns as follows:

6. I ask, unknowing, those who know, the sages, as one all ignorant for sake of knowledge,
    What was that ONE who in the Unborn's image hath established and fixed firm these worlds' six regions?
7. Let him who knoweth presently declare it, this lovely Bird's securely founded station.
    Forth from his head the Cows draw milk, and, wearing his vesture, with their foot have drunk the water.
8. The Mother gave the Sire his share of Order: with thought, at first, she wedded him in spirit.
    She, the coy Dame, was filled with dew prolific: with adoration men approached to praise her.
9. Yoked was the Mother to the boon Cow's car-pole: in the dank rows of cloud the Infant rested.
    Then the Calf lowed, and looked upon the Mother, the Cow who wears all shapes in three directions.
10. Bearing three Mothers and three Fathers, single he stood erect: they never make him weary.

There on the pitch of heaven they speak together in speech all-knowing but not all-impelling.

11. Formed with twelve spokes, by length of time, unweakened, rolls round the heaven this wheel of during Order.

Herein established, joined in pairs together, seven hundred Sons and twenty stand, O Agni.

12. They call him in the farther half of heaven the Sire five-footed, of twelve forms, wealthy in watery store. These others say that he, God with far-seeing eyes, is mounted on the lower seven-wheeled, six-spoked car.

13. Upon this five-spoked wheel revolving ever all living creatures rest and are dependent.

Its axle, heavy-laden, is not heated: the nave from ancient time remains unbroken.

14. The wheel revolves, unwasting, with its felly: ten draw it, yoked to the far-stretching car-pole. The Sun's eye moves encompassed by the region: on him dependent rest all living creatures.[51]

Vishnu, as invoked in these hymns, is the supreme energy that sustains the world. The Vedic trinity—Brahma, Vishnu, and Mahesh—is marked by the cosmic responsibilities they carry, which are, respectively, the creation, preservation, and destruction of the universe. All three have, in some symbolic

---

[51]Griffith (trans.), *The Rig Veda*, 'HYMN CLXIV, Visvedevas', *Sacred Texts*, <www.sacred-texts.com/hin/rigveda/rv01164.htm> [accessed: 1 July 2021].

representation or another, an association with the wheel. Brahma or Prajapati is till this day associated with the potter's wheel. Mahesh or Shiva is shown in his ultimate cosmic unity as androgynous Ardhanari Nateshwar and is iconographically shown as the Lord of the giant wheel of Kala. Vishnu, among the three, has the most intimate association with the wheel. His is the wheel of Time, the kala chakra, which has twelve spokes. The kala chakra, indicating the inexorable flow of events in human time, is at the very heart of the *Mahabharata*.

The wheel motif appears once again in a powerful and evocative visual form in the ancient sculpture at Sarnath. The dhamma chakra brings the wheel of the kala purusha, one of the main deputies of Yama, the god of death, to meet the philosophical reflections of the Buddha. As mentioned in the last paragraph, the symbolic significance of chakra as Time, kala, predates both the *Mahabharata* and the Buddha. However, it does not go back just to the *Rig Veda*, but much beyond it to the times when the Sanskrit language existed in the form of Indo-Iranian, a period several hundred years before the emergence of Indic or Vedic Sanskrit. The term 'chakra' has been traced to the language or languages considered to be the ancestors of both Sanskrit and Pali. Several other languages that are believed to have arisen out of the proto-Indo-European—an ancestor of many of the major languages of the 'ancient world'—including Latin, Greek, Sanskrit, and Turkish.

Historical linguistics tells us that 'there was probably a word *"kwekwlos"*, meaning "wheel", which is the ancestor of *"kuklos"* in classical Greek, of *"kakra"* in Old Indic and—because "k" shifts to "h" in Germanic languages—of *"hweohl"* in Old English, itself the ancestor of "wheel" in modern English.'[52] Thus, 'wheel' or 'chakra' has been in use in the conceptual world of those who spoke the earliest form of Greek, Indic, and Germanic languages. It is a concept older than these languages and inherited from an earlier time, an earlier culture, and an earlier language. David Anthony's *The Horse, The Wheel, and Language* describes the historical transition from pre-chariot warfare to warfare in the era of speedy chariots pulled by powerful horses. For raising kingdoms, gaining superiority in combat, and building empires, horse-driven chariots became so important some thirty-eight centuries before our time that it was but natural for the people of those times to imagine and invest supernatural power in the wheel.

We need to look at the Vedic trinity in the light of this historical context. Brahma, Vishnu, and Mahesh, symbolized as the trinity of the cosmic order, was an idea that marked the pre-*Bharata* centuries. Chariots, whether of Surya, Indra, their Vedic ancestors, or their contemporary warrior kings, acquired a special cultural significance and value in people's minds. The *Bharata* describes the Rajsuya Yagna, a semi-military campaign to establish the Kuru empire during which horses of exceptional majesty were paraded as a military challenge to all adversaries, and during which Krishna uses his chakra to support the challenging clan. The dharma of the *Mahabharata*

---

[52]Nicholas Wade, 'The Tangled Roots of English', *New York Times*, 23 February 2015.

is the dharma of the chakra—the *Mahabharata* is about the dharma chakra. It is not the dhamma of the Buddha, or the dharma of the Brahminical order of ritual-conductors. In it, Arjuna, who alone can lift and wield the Kindhura dhanushya, the divine bow given by Shiva to king Drupad for use in the Draupadi-svayamvar, the contest of heroes to win Draupadi's hand in marriage, represents Shiva. And, despite being the sharpest shooter of arrows unmatched by any other man of his time, at least on occasions, he dances or feels enfeebled by the loss of his masculinity, like the Ardhnari Nateshwara. One such occasion is during the year of anonymity, when he wears the garb of a woman and assumes the name Bruhannada. The second occasion is when he tells Krishna at the beginning of the war that he was smitten by klaibya, loss of manliness. The third such occasion is when fighting with Bhishma, he hides behind Shikhandi, a semi-man-semi-woman character. It is only then that he is able to defeat Bhishma. Thus, the hero who could put strings on Shiva's bow turns to the Nataraja in his destructive mode. There are other mythological references too to the Arjuna–Shiva symbolism, such as in the battle between Kirat and Arjuna. Kirat is the name of a community residing in the eastern Himalayas. Arjuna, who wanted a certain weapon of war from Shiva, was tested by the god who appears in the guise of a Kirat king and challenges Arjuna to prove his war skills. The episode is presented in the Mahabharata in the *Vana Parva* part of the epic.

The horse and the wheel, held high in the collective memory of the later Vedic society, appears in symbolic form in the *Mahabharata* again and again. Karna, despite being the most courageous and committed warrior, is reduced to naught when a wheel of his chariot sinks in the ground. He then climbs down to continue his combat. But without the horses and without the wheels, he loses his battle and dies in combat. Dharma, that is Yudhishthira, is constantly mindful of the kala chakra. He, as we have seen, is the child of Yama, who is considered in that mythology as being Kala himself. The *Mahabharata* war is, at one highly significant level of symbolism, the war for maintaining the kala chakra in its perpetual motion. To that extent, it is an epic of India, that is Bharat. However, it is not a war about preserving or promoting the ritualistic dharma that the later-day *Dharmasutras* codified.

The dharma chakra symbolism seen in the *Mahabharata* had a much wider acceptance in metaphysical schools other than the post-Vedic period Brahminism as well. It was a concept that received legitimacy in ancient Indian political life. The most respected and most powerful king came to be described as a 'chakravarti'. The Sanskrit term 'chakravarti' in its literal sense means the one who can keep the chakra in motion. Buddhist tradition believes that the Buddha will return to the world in the form of a chakravarti. Theravada Buddhist iconography depicts the chakravarti king with a protective ring or chakra above his head.

It is believed that once a chakravarti emerges, the 'future Buddha', Maitreya, would appear on earth. In early Buddhist art there are more than thirty depictions, all from the Deccan, of this avatar of the Buddha. In most of them, the chakravarti uses the 'royal gesture' in which the king clenches his left hand at his chest and reaches up with his right hand. He is surrounded by his seven attributes: the chakraratna, or the wheel, the royal elephant, the steed ready for an attack, the Astapailu, a diamond of divine lustre and having eight facets, the queen, the prime minister, and the minister in charge of treasure. The early Buddhist *Mahavastu* and the *Divyavadana*, as well as the *Theravada Milindapanha*, describe the marks of the chakravarti as ruler: ushnisha, chhatra, or parasol, horn jewel or vajra, whisk, and sandals. These were the marks of the Kshatriya. Plastic art of early Mahayana Buddhism illustrates bodhisattvas in a form called ushnisha, wearing a turban/hair binding, wielding the mudras for non-violent chakravarti rule.

A chakravarti king is one who rules all of the great continents on land, and islands in oceans in all known parts of the earth. He is someone who has brought many kingdoms under his rule through peaceful means. Whenever he travels, the sky starts showing the chakraratna, a divinely ordained natural sign of blessing specially in recognition of the virtue of the chakravarti. It accompanies the king and his army wherever they move, as he travels the world and teaches all kings how to rule with peace. He can travel to regions that ordinary mortals can never reach by using the magical power of the chakraratna. A chakravarti king emerges in history only when humans are virtuous and healthy. The Jataka tales, a part of the Pali Canon, describe Buddhist chakravarti kings.

The concept of dharma chakra also found favour with the Jain tradition of historiography. Jinasena, a major Jain thinker and writer of the Rashtrakuta period, wrote a text during the ninth century quite akin to Vyasa's *Mahabharata*. This text, known as *Harivamsha*, focuses primarily on the Krishna–Jarasandha story. Generally considered as the Jain *Mahabharata*, it does not place the Pandavas at the centre of the plot. It is concerned more with distinguishing the characters into two categories, the baladevas, those who use violence, and the vasudevas, those who desist from using violence. Drawing upon the Jain advocacy of non-violence as a virtue, the concept of chakravarti in Jainism is an emperor who rules through non-violence. Jain cosmology mentions several chakravartis who keep appearing in the world in a cyclic rhythm: Bharata, son of Tirthankara Rishabhanatha; Samara, ancestor of Bhagiratha as in the Puranas; Maghava Sanatkumara; Tirthankara Shantinatha; Tirthankara Kunthunatha; Tirthankara Aranatha; Subhaum; Padmanabha; Harishena; Jayasena; and Brahmadat.

One can see a general acceptance of dharma across faiths, spiritual traditions, and formal faiths as a normative responsibility of emperors, dharma not as a moral order but rather as a cosmic balance of elements. The perpetually moving chakra, therefore, was its best expression, acceptable to all faiths in ancient India. As a powerful statement of this general acceptance of the idea of the emperor's responsibility, Emperor Asoka installed the dharma chakra at Sarnath as his assurance to the people that he would tread the path of dhamma non-violently, as the Jains of his time would have liked him to affirm.

The acceptance of the Sarnath pillar, with the three lions and the kala chakra, as independent India's emblems was a conscious decision to uphold in modern times the ancient Indian principles of inclusiveness and non-violence. Post-Independence India's acceptance of the symbols shows how central the iconography is to the world view of most Indians. The greatest success of the *Mahabharata* lies in bringing in and making alive two powerful symbols, the wheel and the horse. The epic gathered the cultural past spread over a millennium or more, articulated it through powerful symbols, and, thanks to the choice of symbols that dominate the epic, made it relevant for future generations.

VARNA, NATION, AND THE EPIC

The method that the *Mahabharata* employs for bringing together recollections of a vast historical span, beginning with the era when the wheel and the horse were brought together for combats to the times when conflicts between aspiring kingdoms had become the order of the day—a period close to a millennium—makes it necessary for the poet to present long genealogical inventories. Readers will see in the Appendix to this book how the *Sambhava Parva* lists names of mythological figures known in Vyasa's time, including half-forgotten names of remote ancestors, clan lords, and teachers of a time that could be described as 'historical' from Vyasa's perspective. That is quite a catalogue of names. In the process, Vyasa does not forget to mention the ancestors of numerous animal species and plants. Together, they constitute the process of genesis and cosmology as he knew it. He stops mentioning these names when he comes to Abhimanyu. At that point, his tone changes, and the tense used in the verse shifts. He introduces Abhimanyu through prophecy, a common feature of all epics, giving us the impression that the past and the present are merging at a decisive point and the future is about to begin:

> The god Soma had said these words to the celestials, 'I cannot give (part with) my son. He is dearer to me than life itself. Let this be the compact and let it be not transgressed. The destruction of the Asuras on earth is the work of the celestials, and, therefore, it is our work as well. Let this Varchas, therefore, go thither, but let him not stay there long. Nara, whose companion is Narayana, will be born as Indra's son and indeed, will be known as Arjuna, the mighty son of Pandu. This boy of mine shall be his son and become a mighty car-warrior in his boyhood. And let him, ye the best of immortals, stay on earth for sixteen years. And when he attaineth to his sixteenth year, the battle shall take place in which all who are born of your portions shall achieve the destruction of mighty warriors. But a certain encounter shall take place without both Nara and Narayana (taking any part in it). And, indeed, your portions, ye celestials, shall fight, having made that disposition of the forces which is known by the name of the *Chakra-vyuha*. And my son shall compel all foes to retreat before him. The boy of mighty arms having penetrated the impenetrable array, shall range within it fearlessly and send a fourth part of the hostile force, in course of half a day, unto the regions of the king of the

dead. Then when numberless heroes and mighty car-warriors will return to the charge towards the close of the day, my boy of mighty arms, shall reappear before me. And he shall beget one heroic son in his line, who shall continue the almost extinct Bharata race.'[53]

In order to make his genealogies credible, Vyasa has to offer some connecting links such as the 'cause' for the continuation of the line he mentions. Providing causality, convincing or not, is a historian's compulsion; and the *Bharata* was intended to be history. Vyasa, the author of the *Mahabharata*, also faithfully follows the line. Critics have pointed out that the original *Bharata* did not have the *Adi Parva* and that it is a later addition, in all likelihood, by Vyasa. The extended genealogies are thus among Vyasa's contributions to the epic. In them, the details pertaining to the remote past give us the impression that society was still not saddled with the ideas of varna and jati. But the closer we come to the Kuru clan, varna starts becoming a social marker in Vyasa's historiography. Thus Ishupa, an Asura, could become the monarch Nagnajita after coming to Earth; and another Asura, Ekachakra, became Pritivindhya. Closer to the times of the *Bharata*, however, Kshatriyas beget and marry only Kshatriyas. The fear of kula kshaya—bastardization—is a pervasive fear haunting the best among the heroes of the 'war generation'. The war debate, the *Gita*, in the *Bhishma Parva* opens with a clear statement of that fear. Arjuna could have put forth many arguments about the undesirability

---

[53] K. M. Ganguli (trans.), 'Sambhava Parva', LXVII, *The Mahabharata*.

of war. But the only argument he produces is '*kulakshaye pranashyanti kuladharmah sanatanah*'. The verses 36 to 46 of the first adhyaya of the *Gita* are good poetry but problematic politics for a man who is poised to fight a great war for bringing the diverse peoples and kingdoms of the Gangetic plains into a new political system to create an empire. At the commencement of the Kurukshetra war, Arjuna is saying to his charioteer, Krishna:

> O Janardana, what happiness shall we derive by killing the sons of Dhritarashtra? Sin alone will accrue to us by killing these felons. Therefore, it is not proper for us to kill the sons of Dhritarashtra who are our own relatives. For, O Madhava, how can we be happy by killing our kinsmen? O Janardana, although these people, whose hearts have become perverted by greed, do not see the evil arising out of destroying the family and sin in hostility towards friends, yet how can we who clearly see the evil arising out of destroying the family remain unaware of the need for abstaining from sin? From the ruin of the family are totally destroyed the traditional rites and duties of the family. When rites and duties are destroyed, vice overpowers the entire family also. O Krishna, when vice predominates, the women of the family become corrupt. O descendent of the Vrishnis, when women become corrupted, it results in the intermingling of castes. And the intermingling in the family leads the ruins of the family verily into hell. The forefathers of these fall down because of being

deprived of rice-balls and water. Due to these misdeeds of the ruiners of the family, which cause intermingling of castes, the traditional rites and duties of the castes and families become destroyed.... What a pity that we have resolved to commit a great sin by being eager to kill our own kith and kin, out of greed for the pleasure of a kingdom![54]

Arjuna says this despite knowing that his wife Draupadi shares all five Pandava brothers as her husbands. That his mother had given birth to four children from four different progenitors; his father, Pandu, and uncle, Dhritarashtra, were born of Vyasa, who was not exactly of his own kula, or clan; and his great-grandfather, Shantanu, had married women not from the Kshatriya kula, do not fit well in the story of the *Bharata*. The original heroic poem depicts the war fought at the end of a phase of history that brought about the most productive mix of the peoples of India. These included people from local tribes, agriculturalists spread out from the South, descendants of the society that had created Sindhu culture—people who had created a new language, better methods of warfare, and a different pastoral culture. Given the heroism of Arjuna, his courage and fortitude, and considering the profound wisdom of the original composer of *Bharata,* it is most probable that the fear of kula sankara, the mixing of blood and genes, is a latter-day fear brought into the epic when the compendious *Mahabharata* was written, or even much later when the *Gita* was incorporated into the

[54]Gambhirananda (trans.), *Bhagavad Gita*, pp. 25–27.

Mahabharata corpus. Still, despite the history of its evolution as a text, the questions that twenty-first century audiences or readers of the *Mahabharata* are likely to ask are, 'Does it justify discriminatory social practices? And, if it does, can we continue to regard it as a national epic?'

These are harsh questions; and often such questions are not asked of older texts, such as the Vedas or Upanishads or the *Mahabharata*, from the perspective of latter-day assumptions. It is true that a poet works within his own cultural context and ideas of justice keep evolving continuously. Yet, the greatest literary works in the world do stand to this kind of anachronistic scrutiny if it is carried out with the necessary empathy to the work being examined. Let us, therefore, explore what that empathetic approach can be in the context of the *Mahabharata*. The ideal way of exploring that approach is to begin with first applying the most critical view, and then to see if the work deserves to be seen through a less severe lens. I shall, therefore, begin with the comments made by one of the most erudite and thought-provoking leaders of India in the twentieth century, Dr B. R. Ambedkar, a leader whose humanitarian contribution to Indian society is no less than that of Gautama Buddha. In *Annihilation of Caste,* he writes:

> Chaturvarnya is not new. It is as old as the Vedas. That is one of the reasons why we are asked by the Arya Samajists to consider its claim. Judging from the past, as a system of social organization it has been tried, and it has failed. How many times the Brahmins have

annihilated the seed of the Kshatriyas! How many times have the Kshatriyas annihilated the Brahmins! The Mahabharata and the Puranas are full of incidents of the strife between the Brahmins and the Kshatriyas....

Not only was the Brahmin an eyesore to the Kshatriya and the Kshatriya an eyesore to the Brahmin, it seems that the Kshatriyas had become tyrannical, and the masses, disarmed as they were under the system of chaturvarnya, were praying to almighty god for relief from the tyranny. The Bhagwat tells us very definitely that Krishna had taken avatar for one sacred purpose: and that was, to annihilate the Kshatriyas.[55]

In the *Adi Parva* of the *Mahabharata,* such indeed is the explanation for Krishna's life mission, and the *Gita* too expounds on Krishna's mission in life. Besides, there is little to dispute Dr Ambedkar's comments on the history of feuds among different communities in India in the past. That inter-caste, inter-varna tussle can be seen in our time too. *Annihilation of Caste* was expressly written with the purpose of exposing the damages that caste discrimination has caused to Indian society and for exposing the utter fallacy that the foundation this discrimination rests on, which is the caste and varna system. It was not an essay meant to offer comments on the poetic greatness or stylistic brilliance of any ancient literary work. Therefore, his analysis does precisely what it is expected to do. There is, however, an analysis

---

[55]B. R. Ambedkar, *Annihilation of Caste: The Annotated Critical Edition,* New Delhi: Navayana, 2014, pp. 276–77.

that Dr Ambedkar offers which the modern readers of the *Mahabharata* need to consider with utmost seriousness. That comment is about Hindu society's status as a 'nation'. He argues that because of the exclusionary obsession with caste, the Hindu society was not able to become a nation. I quote him at length since there is an important question arising out of his comment about the *Mahabharata*'s historic claim:

> Caste does not result in economic efficiency. Caste cannot improve, and has not improved, race. Caste has, however, done one thing. It has completely disorganised and demoralised the Hindus.
>
> The first and the foremost thing that must be recognised is that Hindu society is a myth. The name Hindu is itself a foreign name. (There is a footnote here mentioning how Al-Biruni's Tarikh al-Hind first used the descriptive tag in AD 1017). It was given by the Mahomedans to the natives for the purpose of distinguishing themselves. They did not feel the necessity of a common name, because they had no conception of having constructed a community. Hindu society as such does not exist. It is only a collection of castes. Each caste is conscious of its existence. Its survival is the be-all and end-all of its existence. Castes do not even form a federation. A caste has no feeling that it is affiliated to other castes, except when there is a Hindu-Moslem riot.
>
> There is an utter lack among the Hindus of what the sociologists call 'consciousness of kind' (there is a note explaining that the phrase was first formed by

the American sociologist Franklin Henry Giddings in 1896). There is no Hindu consciousness of kind. In every Hindu the consciousness that exists is the consciousness of his caste. That is the reason why the Hindus cannot be said to form a society or a nation.[56]

There is nothing at all that I wish to say in defence of the caste system. I have personally refused to be bound by caste throughout my life and have tried in every way possible to go beyond caste and creed and to fight the many forms of injustice that they create. I am in agreement with Dr Ambedkar's argument that a caste-driven society can rarely show the qualities of a 'nation-society'. The observation I would like to bring into consideration here is 'Does the *Mahabharata* have a different concept of nation? And is it because of that concept of the nation that it has continued to resonate with its readership/audiences across centuries?' These questions are not raised in order to absolve the caste system of the charges that Dr Ambedkar makes against them. Those are legitimate charges. These questions are raised to see if in answering them we can shed some light on the nature of the bond that the epic has with our society. Towards that end, it is useful to refer to the 'riddle of life' which occurs at the culmination of the twelve-year exile in the forest imposed on the Pandavas. The riddle is known, with a pun on the word 'yaksha', as the 'yaksha prashna', meaning difficult existential or metaphysical issues. In this instance, they are asked by a Yaksha who is, it turns out at the end of the discussion,

---

[56]Ibid., pp. 241–43.

Yudhishthira's father, Yama.

The story goes as follows: as the Pandava brothers are discussing their plans at the end of the twelve-year sentence of exile, a mendicant approaches them and complains that a certain mysterious deer is obstructing his pursuits. Nakula is sent to deal with the mysterious deer. Wandering far, he notices a beautiful lake and a solitary crane by its side. The crane says to Nakula, 'Do not drink this water without answering my questions, otherwise it will become poison.' He ignores the warning, drinks the water from the lake, and falls dead. Having waited for Nakula, Yudhishthira sends Sahadeva to look for him. He meets with the same end. Then, Arjuna and Bhima follow. When none of them return, Yudhishthira himself goes in their search, arrives at the lake, and sees the corpses of his four brothers and the solitary crane. But, unlike his brothers, he answers the crane's questions. After he has answered those difficult questions, the yaksha prashnas, the crane reveals to Yudhishthira that he is Yama, his father, and brings all his brothers back to life. While the other questions are related to one's attachment to oneself, filial duty, duties towards one's community and one's rajya, the most important question is: Who makes the sun rise, who makes it move forward, who makes it set, and what is the real nature of the sun? Yudhishthira's answer is: 'Brahma makes the sun rise and ascend in the skies, the gods help the sun in making its orbit, and Dharma causes the sunset. Truth is the essence of the sun; and in absence of Truth the sun has no existence.'[57] Other questions follow, and in answering those, Yudhishthira relegates all other identities of man to their limited functional or social realms and places the pursuit of Truth as the supreme duty and identity of humans. This is a lofty thought and has a universal moral value transcending time and place. Yet, is the *Mahabharata* all about Truth, or about metaphysics alone, or is it a defence of the varna system, a glorification of Brahminism? Is it some kind of a twin of the *Manusmriti,* which became the doctrine for the worst consolidation of social discrimination, with the only difference being that the *Mahabharata* is cast in a poetic form? These questions deserve consideration, though they too are as complex as the yaksha prashnas.

The oral *Bharata*, as I have argued earlier, comes at the end of an era extending over nearly a millennium that witnessed the great historical mixing of the Indian population. The larger *Mahabharata* comes at a time when India had gone through a great philosophical contestation that extended over almost a millennium. During that long time, the subcontinent had seen Buddhism and Jainism taking on the consolidated ritualism of the post-*Rig Veda* era. The most contentious metaphysical and moral issues in this great debate were the nature of reality, ethical responsibilities of man, ahimsa or non-violence, and, of course, the essence of life. The *Bharata* invented a method for bringing all strands of the past together, the method that the poem called itihasa, making myth the vehicle for stitching together various

---

[57] K. M. Ganguli (trans.), 'Vana Parva', CCCX, *The Mahabharata.*

stretches of time in that long past. The larger *Mahabharata* was a compendium skilfully versed, great in its meter, caesuras, syllabic combinations (sandhis), and generous in detail. But its primary loyalty remained with the older narrative poem rather than the times in which the larger version was being composed. Thus, it remained shy of the philosophical and metaphysical debates that had been taking place in the centuries preceding its composition. It focused more on warfare, military tactics, political pulls and pushes, and depiction of individual characters. Its hesitation in engaging with the great metaphysical and theological tussles of its times led to it becoming less aggressive in addressing the growing orthodoxy of the post-*Rig Veda* ritualistic idea of dharma. This had a profound effect on the course of the *Mahabharata* throughout the history of India.

It needs to be remembered that the times during which the larger *Bharata*, that is the *Mahabharata* with a hundred thousand verses, was composed were the times when some of the most definitive cultural texts of ancient India were being written in the Sanskrit language. Within the matter of some four or five centuries, thinkers, scholars, and pundits of the day had produced the *Ashtadhyayi* (Panini), *Varttika* (Katyayana), *Mahabhashya* (Patanjali), *Arthashastra* (Kautilya), *Ramayana* (Valmiki), *Natyashastra* (Bharata), and *Madhyamakavatara* (Chandrakirti). This list can be very long. The latter-day Upanishads were emerging and the Puranas were soon to follow. The *Dharmasutras* were driving the process of consolidation of the Brahminical, ritualistic Vedic dharma. The Jains were producing significant literature and Buddhism had already reached lands outside India, after receiving an unprecedented level of political patronage from the times of Emperor Ashoka. Within this context, the prolific poet of the *Mahabharata* had to craft his epic based on the previously existing *Bharata*. Literature in his times was classified as mantra, sutra, shastra, and Suta literature. Kautilya's work on politics was shastra, as was Bharata's work on drama. As against this, the *Mahabharata* was, and remained forever, a work of suta literature. Sutas were reciters of poetry, who wandered from place to place and narrated heroic sagas. Their work was non-Brahminical, and hence, looked down upon by the Brahmins engaged in studying the Vedas. The Sutas in ancient India were not exclusively enjoyed by the Brahminical class. Reading, memorizing, or reciting their works was not taboo for non-Brahmins. Therefore, the *Mahabharata* was intended from the time of its composition as a work available for all. Its author, Vyasa, is also ascribed the authorship of a massive verse companion called *Bhagavat* (not to be confused with the *Gita*). In the times after Vyasa, careful rituals came to be associated with the reading of the *Bhagavat*. The audience for it could be non-Brahminical, but the reader had to be from the Brahmin community. As against this, no such elaborate rules were associated with the reading or reciting of the *Mahabharata*. And, thus it became—as did Valmiki's *Ramayana*—an epic for everybody. Between the two, the *Mahabharata* came to be seen as itihasa while the *Ramayan*a came to be seen as kavya, poetry, first. The *Mahabharata* of Vyasa earned this unique distinction, but it had to pay the price of keeping itself aloof from its contemporary times and turning its glance entirely towards the remote past.

Ever since Vyasa's *Mahabharata* came into circulation, generations of Indians have felt compelled to relate to it, to revive it, and to make it their own through different mediums. In a way, it became the non-Brahmin's book of religion, their dharma grantha, not because it made any claim to being a *Dharmasutra* but because it carefully avoided making that claim. The canonical *Dharmasutras* such as the *Manusmriti* became the fountainhead of scorn, hatred, and social exclusion. Their naked advocacy of varna and caste distinction justified in pseudo-theological and legislative styles, their entirely non-forgiving attitude to labour and the classes engaged in labour, their canonization of scorn and inequality, were sure to alienate the non-Brahminical classes. The *Mahabharata*, on the other hand, remained a much-loved text. Its audiences were prepared to overlook the fact that it too spoke of the Kshatriyas and the Brahmins according to the norms of social orthodoxy. But the characters it depicted in hues of myth, grandeur, and heroism provided all classes of the population a space for imagining a society which had women like Kunti and Draupadi, rulers like Bhishma and Yudhishthira, and heroes like Karna and Abhimanyu. The *Mahabharata* became for Indians during the last 2,000 years a veritable mine of ideals of courage, moral truth, and liberation. The *Bhagavad Gita*, which draws heavily upon the Upanishads, too received this kind of response. Generations of Indians read and recited it as a work that teaches the virtues of action, detachment, and devotion, not so much as a work that advocates violence. Living in a society that was marked by severe exclusions based on caste and gender, repressive pollution norms, and taboos instilled by superstition and fear of divine retribution, people deprived of recognition as humans continued to develop a unique affinity towards the heroes and deities valorized in the *Mahabharata*. Sects and cults dedicated to Vishnu, Krishna, and Ganesha grew in significance throughout the first millennium. The influence of the *Mahabharata* has been so pervasive during the last two millennia that presenting merely an outline of it should easily take several volumes.

Among the modern Indian languages, Tamil has been in use since the time Vyasa wrote his *Mahabharata*. Most other Indian languages started emerging as the chosen medium of people's expression around the beginning of the second millennium. Among them, several have rendered the *Bhagavad Gita* or parts of the *Mahabharata*. Scholars of Sanskrit produced written copies of the epic, which people, even in villages, were keen to acquire if they had enough wealth for doing so. When the Bhandarkar Institute was collecting the *Mahabharata* manuscripts, many were found in places which had not been known places of learning. For instance, a handwritten manuscript dating back to 1512 CE was sourced from a small village called Sankheda in Gujarat's tribal belt. It is included in the critical edition as the 'Sankheda Kapoori' version. I have visited Sankheda numerous times for my work related to the Adivasis, and I did not observe any traces of Brahminical or Vedic education.

During the colonial times, the *Mahabharata* and its

Gita made a strong comeback. Leaders as diverse in their ideologies and political persuasions as Lokmanya Tilak, Sri Aurobindo, and Mahatma Gandhi could relate to the *Gita* with equal fervour. It may not be quite off the mark to say that, among other cultural elements, the *Mahabharata* is one significant cultural production that brings Indians together. The diversity of language, land, and life patterns in this country is so vast that no Indian can genuinely relate to all of it. Probably, it is through cultural practices and icons like the *Mahabharata* that we have a sense of being united. But I must immediately add that I am thinking of a peculiar kind of unity, the unity in how we perceive our long past. The original *Bharata* hit upon that method of remembrance of the things past. In that method, the past need not have a definite beginning. It allows for numerous beginnings. The method does not ground historiography in causality, not in 'x, therefore, y' logic. It is rooted in an a priori acceptance of continuity. Recently, I was asked to write about 'the idea of India'. I reproduce here the opening paragraphs of my essay:

> India, that is, Bharat. The beginnings are many. Geological research, at its current theoretical best, places the formation of the Himalayas to a time ten million years ago. The genomic research, which speaks of human population for over forty-five thousand years, has accepted that the spread of the original population in India is from the peninsular south to the west and north. Plant-genetics has determined a period of some nine thousand years before our time for spread of agricultural

practices from Iran to what is now India. Archaeology takes us back to a period at a distance of five millennia for tracing the roots of our civilization. Linguistic and literary history have succeeded in tracking our path back to a period spanning four thousand years. History as we know, based on verifiable evidence, has pieced together an India of the last 2,700 years. The dawn of the Indian civilization thus has several beginnings.[58]

Given the only partially fulfilled quest to know who we are and from where we came, the picture of India prior to the last 2,500 years has so far remained abundantly hazy, generating specious debates that can at best remain inconclusive. These debates are such that no side can be put on the spot as being entirely ill-construed. I shall, therefore, not get into the question of 'the beginning' of the Indian civilization. Rather, I would like to propose that leaving that question perennially open is one of the foundations of the Indian civilization. What we have been as a civilization may be completely altered if we were to arrive at a hypothesis about the remote past that brooks no exception. William Shakespeare's ability to thrive amidst uncertainties was described by John Keats as 'the negative capability', a great compliment by a great poet. If one may use that phrase in our context, one can say that the foundations of our diverse philosophical schools, literary traditions, linguistic cultures, religious faiths, and

---

[58]G. N. Devy, 'Epic, Narrative and Lyric Ideas of India', *Vision for a Nation: Paths and Perspectives*, Aakash Singh Rathod and Ashis Nandy (eds.), Delhi: Vintage Books, 2019.

social practices are almost entirely based on this ability to remain unchallenged by uncertainties, a civilization's great negative capability. It is this quality that informs our attitude to the objective world, the universe of experience, cultural values, and conceptual understanding of reality.

Civilizations, cultures, and societies keep changing, slowly but definitely, from century to century, from one era to the next. It would be not less than impudent to assume that our civilization has remained what it has been all through its long history. Yet, despite the transitions, the Indian civilization shows a remarkable continuity. The Harappan lota-shaped vase still continues to be in use in India though now it is made in stainless steel. The musical notes used even today draw upon what Saranagdeva or Matanga had set as their basic matrix. The semantics of gestures that the *Natyashastra* of Bharata had codified continues to be effective in the present. One may not be incorrect in assuming that a profound belief in the continuity of things marks our philosophy, thought, expression, social fabric, and cultural forms. The village in India, despite the plunder and devastation it has had to face over the past centuries, has held on and not withered away primarily because we believe that continuity is natural and constitutes an abiding law of history. It is probably for the same reason that despite having massive movements aimed at change from century to century, India has not experienced what can be described as a revolution. Invariably, all of the images of India that have emerged within Indian traditions carry a clear mark of these two—the negative capability allowing a sense of ease with the idea of many beginnings, and the faith in an interminable continuity. Without altering the two, India has been imagined in the past in terms of a relatively vast span of time, an epic time; in terms of a long albeit manageable period, a narrative time; and also in terms of focusing on certain periods of history, a lyric time. The three different imaginations of India have their specific flavour and generic flaws but they also have their unique mesmerizing power and captivating idioms. Instances of all three genres can be found in different periods of our composite history.

The most widely known 'epic imagination' of India to be found among ancient texts is embedded in the *Mahabharata*. One is not pointing to its structure as an epic but rather to its epical presentation of the human condition. The narrative imagination is to be found in the edicts of Ashoka, and the lyrical imagination of India can be located in Kalidasa's play *Abhijnana Shakuntala*. The *Mahabharata* depicts several generations and an epoch-making conflict, a breathtaking range of characters and an amazing wealth of wisdom and information on life as it used to be. Western epics follow an unwritten rule in their composition: they begin the action in medias res. The *Mahabharata* refuses to identify any single act or event as the beginning of its narrative. The *Adi Parva* takes us to many different beginnings, from Shantanu's wanderings to Bhishma's accursed celibacy to stories in the lives of mountains, rivers, ghosts, and animals that it is virtually impossible to say where the story begins. Similarly, several parvas after the conclusion of the war, and even beyond the mythical svargarohana—ascension to heaven—indicate that the ever-moving wheel of life knows no ending. In fact, the *Mahabharata* makes the wheel in perpetual motion its central metaphor. For the *Mahabharata*, that movement is the essence of dharma.

The edicts of Ashoka could have presented him like an Alexander, an all-powerful, all-giving sovereign. But they refrain from doing so. He is instead depicted as a 'devanampriya', a human dear to the gods, because he is humble and ready to serve all. That he chose to make the wheel his primary emblem indicates his understanding of the idea of India. The Shakuntala story is a lyrical statement of the same imagination of India. The story begins at once in the Indra loka where Dushyanta is fighting the menace of the rakshasas and in Kanva's ashram where a young Shakuntala is growing up. It does not end, as would a romance play in any Western tradition, with the reunion of Dushyanta and Shakuntala after a tragic separation caused by a temporary lapse of memory. It continues well past that point and presents to us their young son, Bharata, whose name is accepted as one of the two names of our country by the Constitution.

The *Mahabharata* created a unique method of remembering the past. India has internalized that method as the way of preserving its national memory. The *Mahabharata*, in that sense, is our national epic. It is an epic not about the nation, but about our manner of remembering the past. It unites us as a nation through a similarly perceived past, not through a similarly perceived collective self. In that method, there is a great sense of ease with the past because it admits to having many beginnings. The *Mahabharata* spirit is bound to agitate against any jingoistic and unitary sense of the subcontinent as a nation, for it is marked by an immense diversity of every kind. The *Mahabharata* unites us not in any imagined territorial national space; it brings us together in Time, symbolized by the never-stopping kala chakra, the epic's iconic symbol, which teaches us a great spirit of acceptance of *all that is* in complete humility.

TIME: THE KALA

I have suggested that the *Mahabharata* acquired a place in the Indian imagination as a kind of national epic—though imposing the concept of 'nation' on the kingdoms, kings, peoples, and events described in the *Mahabharata* would be an anachronism—owing to its ability to provide a certain method of perceiving the past. It is necessary to state what that unique method was, and why it was that this particular method came to acquire centrality in preference over other methods that may have been prevalent at the time of the rise of the *Mahabharata* as a powerful narrative. History, as scholars define it, is, of course, a science, a method based on 'logically progressing causality' as its backbone. History, in its technical sense, requires presentation of a sequence of events as a series arising out of causes leading to consequences and, in turn, those consequences becoming causes for yet another set of consequences. What is not a consequence, or cannot be construed as such, does not technically have a place in 'history'; and similarly, what is not a cause, or cannot be shown as one, too has no place there. Very clearly, the narrator of the *Mahabharata* does not attempt to present the sequence of events beginning with the birth of Bhishma to the ascension of the heroes to Svarga as bound together merely through causality. The copious role played by divine interventions in the progress of the narrative rules out the possibility of any such 'logical progression' of the story. I do not intend to argue that the narrative in the *Mahabharata* progresses along any such causal path. I would rather like to propose that the *Mahabharata* is an attempt at presenting a history of its own kind, and show how it establishes a 'prehistorical' method of reorganizing the past which is strikingly different from the method of 'history'.

As I have said before, given the enormously long period of human existence, society, civilization, language, and culture in the Indian subcontinent preceding the era during which the *Mahabharata* was composed, it would be quite illogical to assume that there were no pre-*Mahabharata* 'methods' of recalling the past. Scientifically, any language used by a group of humans which has well-established provisions for talking about the past possesses the potential for conceptualizing the pastness of an event; and if the language of that group enables them to represent the past, the given speech community is bound to have, howsoever nascent, an idea of 'pastness', an idea of 'history' of a kind. The question to be raised here is not if the *Mahabharata* presents a history of its own kind but why this kind of history received such widespread acceptance throughout India and continues to remain acceptable over 2,000 years later. What special features of the kind of history the *Mahabharata* employs make it still seem 'reasonable', despite philosophical and conceptual changes taking place in subsequent centuries which made the world depicted in the epic appear 'bygone', old, remote, and dated? A related question that needs to be asked and answered is why this epic particularly acquired an iconic place as representation of the historical memory of India's prehistoric past. When post-Vedic Sanskrit was in ascendency, India had other well-developed languages such as Pali, Tamil, Prakrit, and an ancient variety of what is the present-day Assamiya. The people who spoke those languages too would have their own perspectives of viewing the ascent of the Bharata clan and the historical events surrounding it. Why is it that their memories of the flow of events did not come to acquire the same significance that the *Bharata*, the original bardic account of those events, did?

The political clash between different power-holding classes of Indian society forming the central action in the epic is confined to the northern parts of India. However, even in those times, Indians in the South and Indians in the North were not entirely isolated from each other. Much before the advent of the Indo-Aryan language into India, the seafaring Southerners had links with Sindh and Balochistan. A branch of the Dravidic language family had reached there. We do not know if the Harappan civilization had any definite Dravidian connection but such claims have been made in relation to the language and the yet undeciphered Indus

Valley script.[59] The *Mahabharata* itself depicts characters and kingdoms from the South; and ancient Tamil folklore clearly speaks of the connect between the Northern 'Aryans' from times long before the larger *Mahabharata* was composed. The legendary sage Agastya was one of the more important links in this relation.

> Agastya is the putative author of the first Tamil grammar *Akkatiyam*.... We do not know when Agastya's name was first connected with Tamil grammar. This sage, the last and the most unusual of the so-called seven Vedic sages (saptrashi), is already well known in the Rig Veda, which includes among other references, a dialogue between Agastya and his wife, Lopamudra (I.179). Late Vedic traditions and their reflexes in medieval commentary tell us he was born as a fish in a pot (kumbha) after two gods, Varuna and Mitra, shed their seed in it when they saw the ravishing dancing-girl, Urvasi.... The Sanskrit epics describe the circumstances of his southward excursion: he was sent by the gods to force the Vindhya Mountains, which had risen to the zenith of the cosmos and were interfering with normal cosmic operations, to shrink back to their normal size (Mahabharata 3-102.... Kalidasa links Agastya with the Pandya kingdom of Madurai and its king, at whose horse sacrifice the sage officiated; thus by the late fourth century, if not earlier, classical north Indian

---

[59] Andrew Robinson, *Lost Languages: The Enigma of the World's Undeciphered Scripts*, New York: Thames and Hudson, 2002, pp. 264–94.

sources thought of Agastya as having a south Indian connection—indeed, he was probably pictured as a pioneer of Vedic civilization in the far south.[60]

It must be noted here that the varieties of the past tenses available in Tamil during its early stages differed significantly from the past tense structures available in Sanskrit. The semantic universe of the Tamil language was distributed between the binary of the present and the not present, whereas Sanskrit had a four-layered past tense: the past, the continuous past, the past-past, and an ever-present past. Therefore, the historical memories contained in the Sanskrit oral traditions when the original *Bharata* was composed were bound to be more nuanced and evocative. The entire *Mahabharata* is written in a variety of past tenses, in sentences such as 'having done X, A proceeded to do Y', never forgetting to emphasize, what T. S. Eliot would have called, the 'pastness of the past'.[61] The 'pastness' is underscored by use of the 'perfect past'—'He had done X'—and not by using the simple past—'He did X'. This method was less accessible for the Tamil version of the same 'past' since the Tamil language repertoire for representing it was comparatively less flexible than the Sanskrit.

I am not suggesting that there was, or may have been, a parallel Tamil *Bharata* which may have gradually given way in

---

[60]David Shulman, *Tamil: A Biography*, Cambridge, MA: Harvard University Press, 2016, p. 26.

[61]T. S. Eliot, 'Tradition and Indivual Talent', *The Sacred Wood: Essays on Poetry and Criticism*, London: Methuen Publishing, 1920.

people's memories to the Sanskrit *Bharata*. Researchers so far do not give any indication to such a phenomenon. However, when the search for various manuscripts of *Mahabharata* was carried out leading to the Bhandarkar Institute's critical edition, it was noticed that the manuscripts had survived in a greater abundance in South India than in the North. The larger range of conceptualizing the past available in Sanskrit *may* have been one of the reasons for the fascination for the epic in the South.

In the case of the North-Eastern regions, the Pali language was in use during the period between the emergence of the bardic *Bharata* and the composition of the comprehensive *Mahabharata*. Pali was already a text- and a tense-rich language when the saga of the Kuru clan's war was circulating in oral traditions in India. It is true that Gautama Buddha does not figure in the larger *Mahabharata* which was put together several centuries after the Buddha; and it is also true that Buddhist texts do not mention the *Bharata* war. However, as we have already seen, the contestation between the Vedic ideas and goals of life and Gautama Buddha's ideals of nirvana and collective responsibility was the central theological and philosophical discourse during the centuries spanning the Buddha's life and the composition of the larger *Mahabharata* half a millennium later. The geographical area where the Buddha lived and travelled during his four decades as a wandering philosopher-saint had several living languages in use. The language of Magadha, the ancestor of the present-day Magahi, was only one of them. There were also the ancestors of present-day Assamiya, Bangla, Khasi, Garo,

Manipuri, and Bodo. It is clear from the historical accounts of the Buddha's life, times, travels, and conversations with his disciples that the linguistic apparatus available in these languages was sufficiently competent to allow them to construct and circulate the history that the *Bharata* saga, in existence even before Buddha's birth, contained. Not only were they sufficiently competent to present a complex historical account; some of them in fact gave to the Sanskrit language some of their own linguistic features, making the Sanskrit language more competent than it previously was. Assamese scholar Maheshwar Neog, though broadly following the historical linguistics claims of Suniti Kumar Chatterji, tells us that the tense-sign in the ancient Maghadi, which was closer to Pali, was distinct from contemporary Sanskrit tense forms. After providing an overview of the history of ancient inscriptions in Prakrit and offering various explanations for the code-mixing in the inscriptions, Neog states:

> The literary Prakrits do not record the actual spoken dialects of the various dialect areas; but the literary specimen at least helps us to characterize the process of change and simplification which were going on through the centuries. The comparative survey of all the MIA (Middle Indo Aryan) records beginning from the Proto-Prakrit stage down to the emergence of NIA (Northeast Indo Aryan) is sure to give a vivid and descriptive account of the historical course of the Indo-Aryan. A student working on the growth and development of a modern Aryan language cannot overlook the history

of the development of the MIA (Middle Indo Aryan) dialects. This does not mean, however, that each and every form and feature of our vernacular are traceable to the earlier period; there are innovations, and in the event of falling into disuse and subsequent loss of a syntactic morpheme, a new one may be reconstructed, or a native form might have gained predominance. The future tense sign, --*b*, for example, did not come to the NIA (Northeast Indo Aryan) from its OIA (Old Indo Aryan) counterpart through MIA (Middle Indo Aryan). The Magadhan future sign, --*b*, is, however, based on an OIA (Old Indo Aryan) gerundive (-*tavya*), which was not inherited directly, but through the process of change that had been operating in MIA (Middle Indo Aryan); but this Magadhan tense sign is distinct from its Hindi counterpart.[62]

He then offers a list of 'Prakritisms' in Assamese to substantiate his observation. Neog has been understandably hesitant in pushing the claim that the ancient forms of the eastern languages, now classified as Modern Indo-Aryan languages, have made more substantial contributions to Sanskrit than has so far been acknowledged. Unfortunately, the amount of scholarly attention that the Prakrit languages in India received has not been adequate in comparison to the attention that Sanskrit has received over the last two centuries. Yet, it is now accepted that the Modern Indo-Aryan

---

[62]Maheswar Neog, *Essays on Assamese Literatures*, Guwahati: Omsons Publications, 2004, pp. 26–27.

languages—such as Gujarati, Marathi, Oriya, Bangla, and Assamiya—have evolved from Prakrits in combination with the Sanskrit language. What is more important for us to know here is that even the Sanskrit language has been influenced by the pre-existing Prakrits in India. The influence was by no means one way; it was a mutually enriching exchange, and one that deeply impacted the destiny of India. The extent of the influence of the Prakrits on Sanskrit during its early centuries can become clear when we compare the early Indo-Aryan with its linguistic sister, the early Indo-Iranian.

The Indo-Aryan has an *i/ī* sound representing a Proto-Indo-European laryngeal sound not only in initial syllables but also, generally, in interior syllables, as in Sanskrit *duhitr̥-* 'daughter' (*cf.* Greek *thugátēr*). In Iranian, the original laryngeal is lost in this position, as in Avestan *dugədar-*, *duγδdar-*. Similarly, Sanskrit *bravīti* 'speaks, says,' *vr̥ṇīte* 'chooses,' but Avestan *mraoⁱti*, *vərⁿtē*. Iranian also has replaced Indo-Iranian aspirated voiced consonants (pronounced with a puff of breath, written *h*) with corresponding unaspirated consonants—e.g., Sanskrit *gharma-* 'warmth,' *dhā* 'put, make,' and *bhr̥*, 'carry, bear' but Avestan *garᵊma-* 'warm' and Avestan and Old Persian *dā*, *bar*. Further, Iranian changed stops such as *p* before certain consonants to spirants such as *f*: Sanskrit *pra* 'forth,' Avestan *frā*; Old Persian *fra*; Sanskrit *putra-* 'son,' Avestan *puθra-*, Old Persian *puṣṣa-* (ṣṣ represents a sound that is also transliterated as *ç*). In addition, *h* replaces *s* in Iranian except before non-nasal stops (produced by releasing the breath only through the mouth) and after *i, u, r,* vocalic *r,* and *k;* Avestan *hapta-* 'seven,' *ha^uruua-* 'whole, Old Persian *haruva-* 'whole,' as opposed to Sanskrit *sapta-, sarva.*[63]

The Prakrit languages in India had their own methods of representing history. Some of the best known in the medieval period are the Charani history in Rajasthan, the Buranji in Assamiya, and the Bakhar in Marathi. Among these, the most interesting for any future research in the *Mahabharata* tradition should be the oral history tradition in the western parts of India, particularly the vast desert in Kutch, Rajasthan, and the adjoining Sindh (now in Pakistan). It was in this area that nearly sixteen centuries before the first *Bharata* started circulating in its oral form and nearly twenty-five centuries before the larger *Mahabharata* was compiled that the Indus Valley civilization had flourished. Even after it diminished, human habitation continued in the area. Some day in the future, when scholars succeed in decoding the Indus Valley script, and when more archaeological evidence is gathered, the world will come to know more about this era of Indian history. However, till that happens, it may be of interest to us to note that a different sense of 'history' marks the Prakrit varieties existing in the region. Luigi Pio Tessitori, an Italian folklorist, carried out in his short life

---

[63]'Characteristics of Iranian and Indo-Aryan', *Encylopaedia Britannica,* <https://www.britannica.com/topic/Indo-Iranian-languages/ Characteristics-of-Iranian-and-Indo-Aryan> [accessed: 9 June 2020].

remarkably enriching studies on the bardic traditions in Rajasthan. Tanuja Kothiyal, a contemporary young historian, has thrown light on the cultural significance of the nomadic communities in Rajasthan. Drawing upon Tessitori's *Bardic and Historical Survey of Rajputana* and the Gujarati folklorist Jhaverchand Meghani—particularly their portrayal of the Charani tradition in Dingal linguistic and stylistic variety— Kothiyal observes that the Dingal style could be traced back to Prakrit and Apabhramsha. She further draws attention to the element of 'truth' in the Charani narratives, despite their great stylistic flourishes. She comments:

> Posited against the histories based on dispassionate facts, the *bats* of the Charans were quickly discredited. They were no longer regarded as history but were to be studied in the realm of poetics and linguistics. But we need to question if Charans ever claimed that their work be regarded as 'history'. The desire to see an 'objective' history in the works of the Charans was pointless as the role of the Charans was not of an '"objective" historian, but that of a seer, a guardian of legend, and a conserver of tradition.' He did not consciously manipulate the truth, but represented the truth that he saw, as he himself was a part of that 'truth'. This 'truth' did not associate so much with the objective facts, as it did with the social order and ideal that the Charan endeavored to preserve.[64]

---

[64]Tanuja Kothiyal, *Nomadic Narratives: A History of Mobility and Identity in the Great Indian Desert*, New Delhi: Cambridge University Press, 2016,

In human history, historiographical perspectives have often clashed, one gaining ascendency over other prevailing perspectives. In the first millennium, Roman historians made Greek histories and historical verse narratives look irrelevant. Pliny (34–79 CE) of the first century made Megasthenes (350–290 BCE) look like a mere storyteller and fantasy writer. During the colonial times in India, the royal historians employed by kings were eclipsed by European scholars. Kothiyal's concern is the interface between colonial historiography and the historiography of the immediately preceding era. It would not make sense to project this observation on intellectual culture over a millennium and a half older. One cannot say if Vyasa, to whom the authorship of the larger *Mahabharata* is ascribed, was aware of the oral-history traditions in the western Prakrits. Yet, Kothiyal's characterization of Charani oral history provides us a perspective to view the place of eminence that Vyasa's *Mahabharata* gained in Indian history. 'Truth' of a social order is a valuable historiographical concept when one is dealing with histories other than those based on logical causal-progression within a set chronological order. Sri Aurobindo had suggested that the 'truth' value in the case of such other histories lies in the organic link between what is narrated and the audience for which it is narrated. Commenting on the immense appeal of the *Ramayana* and the *Mahabharata* to the Indian people, he wrote:

> The *Mahabharata* especially is not only the story of the Bharatas, the epic of an early event which had become a

---

p. 230.

national tradition but on a vast scale the epic of the soul and religious and ethical mind and social and political ideals and culture and life of India. It is said popularly of it and with a certain measure of truth that whatever is in India is in the *Mahabharata*. The *Mahabharata* is the creation and expression not of a single individual mind, but of the mind of a nation; it is a poem of itself written by a whole people.[65]

I would like to add to these valuable insights an observation related to the unique treatment of the epic's subject in the *Mahabharata*. As mentioned earlier in the text, Yama in myth and Yudhishthira in the epic are probably the most focal among the plethora of characters depicted in the epic. Equally important is the wheel motif. Taken together, they indicate that kala, Time, is an important preoccupation of Vyasa. He presents Time in several of its aspects: cosmic time, mythical time, historical time, and a psychological time, as in the consciousness of individual characters. In ancient iconography, Ananta, a coiled serpent, represents Time without either a beginning or an end. It advances partly in circular waves and partly in linear moves. The deity governing Ananta is Vishnu. In the cosmology that accepts Ananta as the infinite Time, Krishna is considered a reincarnation of Vishnu. Thus, apart from the human and political character Krishna, one aspect of the Krishna as depicted in the *Mahabharata* relates to cosmic time, whose Lord and Master he is. He is described as the tamer of Kaliya, a diabolic representation of

---

[65]Aurobindo, *The Mahabharata*, p. 167.

Shesha, the cobra on whose body Vishnu rests, according to Puranic mythology. He wields the Sudarshan Chakra and is able to demonstrate to Arjuna on the battlefield the cosmic passage of life and all beings in the past, present, and future.

Time as myth touches the lives of all characters in the epic. Almost all of them are born by mythical incidents and many of them carry boons and curses through their lives, like in myths. Mythical time recognizes no temporality. In it, a character like Vyasa can be present at the beginning of the story being told as well as at its end several generations later, without any physical changes, and a character like Ganga can rise in human space at will and disappear again at will. The schooling of the Kuru princes, their political moves, the exile, return from the forest, and the Kurukshetra war are the events that follow, more or less, the temporal scheme of time as it normally is in heroic narratives, full of hyperbole and yet recognizably within the grasp of a human time scale. Finally, Yudhishthira's encounter with Yaksha, who turns out to be no other than his own father, Arjuna's conversation with Krishna at the beginning of the war, Bhishma's death spread over several months are all depictions of intense psychological fragments of time.

The *Mahabharata* brings all of these four imaginations of Time together. The poet of this remarkable epic works out the magic of welding together the differently imagined Times with such vigour and ease that it is almost impossible for one to segregate them. The seamless stitching together of these different schemes or imaginations of Time is, what I would like to call, the *Mahabharata* method of presenting history, which is never a complete objective truth nor a complete fiction, which is quite outside the realm either of fact or fiction, a universe within itself. If one were to answer the question, 'What is it all about?', one can propose with a fair degree of justice that, apart from it being about many, many other important things, it is about a method of understanding the past as a composite time, an aggregate of all aspects of Time, the kala. The *Mahabharata* gave India this method and it is because of this that Indian people have rarely been able to perceive their past, their histories, in terms other than the ones the *Mahabharata* method has proposed. It is, therefore, also why India has not stopped its lavish adoration of the epic. Despite its depiction of the varna system in a manner that should offend any Indian believing in equality of all humans, despite its foregrounding the idea of rebirth which any modern mind will find untenable, despite its valorization of a social order that almost amounted to a slavery-based society, the *Mahabharata* is yet not regarded by Indian people as a work of the past because it brings to them the *Mahabharata* method of perceiving the past.

REFERENCES

'Characteristics of Iranian and Indo-Aryan', *Encyclopaedia Britannica*, <www.britannica.com/topic/Indo-Iranian-languages/Characteristics-of-Iranian-and-Indo-Aryan> [accessed: 9 June 2020].

Ambedkar, B. R., *Annihilation of Caste: The Annotated Critical Edition*, Introduction by Arundhati Roy, New Delhi: Navayana, 2014.

Anthony, David W., *The Horse, the Wheel, and Language: How Bronze-Age Riders from the Eurasian Steppes Shaped the Modern World*, Princeton and Oxford: Princeton University Press, 2007.

Aurobindo, Sri, *The Mahabharata: Essays and Translations*, Pondicherry: Sri Aurobindo Ashram, 1991, 2019.

Balasubramaniam, R., *Marvels of Indian Iron through the Ages*, Infinity Foundation Series, New Delhi: Rupa Publications, 2008.

Das, Ashok Kumar, *Paintings of the Razmnama: The Book of War*, Ahmedabad: Mapin Publishers, 1985.

Deshpande, Madhav M., 'Aryan Origins: Brief History of Linguistic Arguments', in Romila Thapar et al., *India: Historical Beginnings and the Concept of the Aryan*, New Delhi: National Book Trust, 2013.

Eswaran, Eknath, introduction and trans., *The Dhammapada*, New Delhi: Penguin Books India, 1986.

Gambhirananda, Swami, trans., *Bhagavad Gita: With the Commentary of Shankaracharya*, Kolkata: Swapna, 1991.

Ganguli, K. M., trans., *The Mahabharata of Krishna-Dwaipayana Vyasa: translated into English Prose from the Original Sanskrit Text*, 1883–1896, <archive.org/details/TheMahabharataOfKrishna-dwaipayanaVyasa/mode/2up>.

Griffith, Ralph T. H., trans., *The Rig Veda*, 1896, Sacred Texts, <www.sacred-texts.com/hin/rigveda> [accessed: 1 July 2021].

Kenoyer, Jonathan Mark, 'Cultures and Societies of the Indian Tradition', in Romila Thapar et al., *India: Historical Beginnings and the Concept of the Aryan*, New Delhi: National Book Trust, 2013.

Kothiyal, Tanuja, *Nomadic Narratives: A History of Mobility and Identity in the Great Indian Desert*, New Delhi: Cambridge University Press, 2016.

Neog, Maheswar, *Essays on Assamese Literatures*, Guwahati: Omsons Publications, 2004.

Olivelle, Patrick, trans., *Dharmasutras: The Law Codes of Ancient India*, New Delhi: Oxford University Press, 1999.

Patil, Sharad, *Caste Feudal Servitude*, Shirur: Mavalai Prakashan, 2006.

Radhakrishnan, S., *The Principal Upanishads: Edited with Introduction, Text, Translation and Notes*, New Delhi: Oxford University Press, 1953, 1990.

Reich, David, *Who We Are and How We Got Here: Ancient DNA and the New Science of the Human Past*, New York: Pantheon Books, 2018.

Robinson, Andrew, *Lost Languages: The Enigma of the World's Undeciphered Scripts*, New York: Thames and Hudson, 2002.

Shulman, David, *Tamil: A Biography*, Cambridge, MA: Harvard University Press, 2016.

Tilak, Bal Gangadhar, *Orion: Or Researches into the Antiquity of the Vedas*, Pune: Geeta Printers, 1893, 1999.

Note: *The Critical Edition of the Mahabharata*, a project of the Bhandarkar Oriental Research Institute, Pune, spread over several decades, and edited by Bhandarkar, Belvalkar, and Sukhathankar in different times has resulted in a version of the *Mahabharata* spanning nineteen volumes (twenty-two books) which offers a comparative and critical version of the *Mahabharata*. The volumes originally published by the Bhandarkar Institute were re-published in a single set edition by Penguin in 2019.

GENEALOGY PRESENTED IN THE
MAHABHARATA

Note: *Readers need not consider this genealogy as a historical record. This genealogy is to give the readers an idea of how the* Mahabharata *viewed the succession of past epochs, as presented in Book 1:* Adi Parva, *Canto and* Sambhava: *Sections LXVI and LXVII, making a seamless combination of myth and history the frame of reference for the plot of the epic.*

GODS AND PERSONIFIED VIRTUES

There are thirty-three celestial beings in the genealogy: the eight Vasus, the eleven Rudras, the twelve Adityas, Prajapati, and Vashatkara.

The spiritual sons of Brahman: the six great Rishis Marichi, Angiras, Atri, Pulastya, Pulaha, Kratu, and a seventh one named Sthanu.

The sons of Sthanu were eleven: Mrigavayadha, Sarpa, Niriti, Ajaikapat, Ahivradhna, Pinaki, Dahana, Iswara, Kapali, Sthanu, Bharga.

These are called the eleven Rudras.

Angiras' three sons: Vrihaspati, Utathya, and Samvarta.

The sons of Atri are numerous.

The sons of Pulastya: Rakshasas, monkeys, kinnaras (half-men and half-horses), and Yakshas.

The son of Pulaha: Salabhas (winged insects), lions, kimpurushas (half-lions and half-men), tigers, bears, wolves.

The sons of Kratu: the companions of Surya.

The Rishi Daksha, sprung from the right toe of Brahman.

And from the left toe of Brahman sprang the wife of the high-souled Daksha. And the Muni begat upon her fifty daughters, his putrikas (so that *their* sons might belong both to himself and to their husbands).

Daksha bestowed ten of his daughters on Dharma: Kirti, Lakshmi, Dhriti, Medha, Pushti, Sraddha, Kria, Buddhi, Lajja, and Mali; twenty-seven on Chandra, the Nakshatras; and thirteen on Kasyapa.

Brahman had another son named Manu. And Manu had a son of the name of Prajapati. The sons of Prajapati were eight and were called Vasus: Dhara, Dhruva, Soma, Aha, Anila, Anala, Pratyusha, and Prabhasa.

Dhara and the truth-knowing Dhruva were born of Dhumra.

Chandramas (Soma) and Swasana (Anila) were born of the intelligent Swasa, Aha was the son of Rata, Hutasana (Anala) of Sandilya, and Pratyusha and Prabhasa were the sons of Prabhata.

Dhara had two sons: Dravina and Hutahavyavaha.

The son of Dhruva is the illustrious Kala (Time), the destroyer of the worlds. Soma's son is the resplendent Varchas.

Varchas and his wife Manohara had the sons Sisira and Ramana.

The sons of Aha were Jyotih, Sama, Santa, and Muni.

The son of Agni is Kumara, born in a forest of reeds, called Kartikeya.

Agni has three more sons: Sakha, Visakha, and Naigameya.

The wife of Anila is Shiva.

Shiva's sons were Manojava and Avijnataagati.

The son of Pratyusha is the Rishi named Devala.

Devala had two sons who were both forgiving and of great mental power.

The sister of Vrihaspati, the first of women, uttering the sacred truth, roamed over the whole earth; and she became the wife of Prabhasa, the eighth Vasu.

Prabhasa and Vrihaspati gave birth to Viswakarman, the founder of all arts.

Dharma, the dispenser of all happiness, came out through the right breast of Brahman.

Dharma hath three excellent sons: Sama, Kama, and Harsha.

The wife of Kama is Rati.

The wife of Sama is Prapti.

The wife of Harsha is Nanda.

The son of Marichi is Kasyapa.

Kasyapa's offspring are the Suras and the Asuras. Thus, he is the Father of the worlds.

Tvashtri, the wife of Savitri (Surya), gave birth to greatly fortunate twins, the Ashwins.

The sons of Aditi are twelve, with Indra heading them all.

The youngest of them was Vishnu.

◆

The illustrious Bhrigu came out, ripping open the breast of Brahman.

The learned Sukra is Bhrigu's son.

And Sukra divided himself in two by the power of asceticism

and became the spiritual guide of both the Daityas and the gods. And after Sukra was thus employed by Brahman, Bhrigu begot another son. This was Chyavana.

And Arushi, the daughter of Manu, became his wife.

Their son was Aurva.

Aurva begot Richika.

Richika begot Jamadagni.

Jamadagni had four sons, the youngest of them all was Rama/Parasurama.

Parasurama became the slayer of the Kshatriyas.

Aurva had a hundred sons with Jamadagni. And these hundred sons had offspring by thousands spread over this earth. Brahman had two other sons, Dhatri and Vidhatri, who stayed with Manu.

Their sister is the auspicious Lakshmi, who has her abode amid lotuses.

The spiritual sons of Lakshmi are the sky-ranging horses.

The daughter born of Sukra, named Divi, became the eldest wife of Varuna.

Of her were born a son named Vala and a daughter named Sura.

Adharma had Niriti for his wife, and they gave birth to Nairitas and also three other cruel sons, Bhaya, Mahabhaya, and Mrityu.

ANIMALS AND PLANTS

Tamra brought forth five daughters known throughout the worlds.

They are Kaki (crow), Syeni (hawk), Phasi (hen),

Dhritarashtri (goose), and Suki (parrot). And Kaki brought forth the crows; Syeni, the hawks, cocks, and vultures; Dhritarashtri all ducks and swans; and she also brought forth all Chakravakas; and the fair Suki, of amiable qualities, and possessing all auspicious signs, brought forth all the parrots. And Krodha gave birth to nine daughters, all of wrathful disposition. And their names were Mrigi, Mrigamanda, Hari, Bhadramana, Matangi, Sarduli, Sweta, Surabhi, and the agreeable Surasa blessed with every virtue. And, O foremost of men, the offspring of Mrigi are all animals of the deer species. And the offspring of Mrigamanda are all animals of the bear species and those called Srimara (sweet-footed). And Bhadramana begot the celestial elephant, Airavata. And the offspring of Hari are all animals of the simian species endued with great activity, so also all the horses. And those animals also, that are called go-langula (the cow-tailed), are said to be the offspring of Hari. And Sarduli begot lions and tigers in numbers, and also leopards and all other strong animals. And Sweta begot the large elephant known by the name of Sweta, endued with great speed. Surabhi gave birth to two daughters, the amiable Rohini and the far-famed Gandharvi. She had also two other daughters named Vimala and Anala. From Rohini have sprung all kine, and from Gandharvi all animals of the horse species. And Anala begat the seven kinds of trees yielding pulpy fruits. (They are the date, the palm, the hintala, the tali, the little date, the nut, and the coconut.) And she had also another daughter called Suki, the mother of the parrot species. And Surasa bore a son called Kanka (a species of long-feathered birds). And Syeni, the wife of Aruna, gave birth to two sons of great energy and strength, named Sampati and the mighty Jatayu. Surasa also bore the Nagas, and Kadru, the Punnagas (snakes). And Vinata had two sons, Garuda and Aruna, known far and wide.

THE SUPERNATURAL AS REPRESENTED AMONG HUMANS

The birth, among men, of the gods, the Danavas, the Gandharvas, the Rakshasas, the lions, the tigers, and the other animals, the snakes, the birds.

The first of Danavas, who was the son of Diti known by the name of Viprachitti, noted as Jarasandha, also known as Hiranyakasipu, was known in this world among men as the powerful Sisupala.

He who had been known as Samhlada, the younger brother of Prahlada, became among men the famous Salya.

The spirited Anuhlada who had been the youngest became noted in the world as Dhrishtaketu.

That son of Diti who had been known as Sivi became on earth the famous monarch Druma.

The great Asura Vashkala became on earth the great Bhagadatta.

The five great Asuras gifted with great energy, Ayahsira, Aswasira, the spirited Aysanku, Gaganamurdhan, and Vegavat, were all born in the royal line of Kekaya and all became great monarchs.

That other Asura of mighty energy who was known by the name of Ketumat became on earth the monarch Amitaujas.

That great Asura who was known as Swarbhanu became on earth the monarch Ugrasena.

That great Asura who was known as Ashwa became on

earth the monarch Ashoka.

The younger brother of Ashwa who was known as Ashwapati, a son of Diti, became on earth the mighty monarch Hardikya.

The great and fortunate Asura who was known as Vrishaparvan became noted on earth as king Dirghaprajna.

The younger brother of Vrishaparvan who was known by the name of Ajaka became noted on earth as king Salwa.

The powerful and mighty Asura who was known as Ashwagriva became noted on earth as king Rochamana.

The Asura who was known as Sukshma, endued with great intelligence, became on earth the famous king Vrihadratha.

And that first of Asuras who was known by the name of Tuhunda, became noted on earth as the monarch Senavindu.

That Asura of great strength who was known as Ishupa became the monarch Nagnajita of famous prowess.

The great Asura who was known as Ekachakra became noted on earth as Pritivindhya.

The great Asura Virupaksha, capable of displaying various modes of fight, became noted on earth as king Chitravarman.

The first of Danavas, the heroic Hara, who humbled the pride of all foes became on earth the famous and fortunate Suvahu.

The Asura Suhtra, of great energy and the destroyer of foemen, became noted on earth as the fortunate monarch Munjakesa.

That Asura of great intelligence called Nikumbha, who was never vanquished in a battle, was born on earth as king Devadhipa, the first among monarchs.

That great Asura known amongst the sons of Diti by the

name of Sarabha became on earth the royal sage called Paurava.

Kupatha was born on earth as the famous monarch Suparswa.

Kratha was born on earth as the royal sage Parvateya of form resplendent like a golden mountain.

Salabha the second became on earth the monarch Prahlada.

Chandra, handsome as the lord of the stars himself, became on earth Chandravarman, the king of the Kamvojas.

That bull amongst the Danavas, who was known by the name of Arka, became on earth the royal sage Rishika.

That best of Asuras who was known as Mritapa became on earth the monarch Pascimanupaka.

That great Asura of surpassing energy known as Garishtha became noted on earth as king Drumasena.

The great Asura who was known as Mayura became noted on earth as the monarch Viswa.

He who was the younger brother of Mayura and called Suparna became noted on earth as the monarch Kalakirti.

The mighty Asura who was known as Chandrahantri became on earth the royal sage Sunaka.

The great Asura who was called Chandravinasana became noted on earth as the monarch Janaki.

That bull amongst the Danavas, who was called Dhirghajihva, became noted on earth as Kasiraja.

The Graha who was brought forth by Sinhika and who persecuted the Sun and the Moon became noted on earth as the monarch Kratha.

The eldest of the four sons of Danayu, who was known by the name of Vikshara, became known on earth the spirited monarch Vasumitra.

The second brother of Vikshara, the great Asura, was born on earth as the king of the country, called Pandya.

That best of Asuras who was known by the name of Valina became on earth the monarch Paundramatsyaka.

That great Asura who was known as Vritra became on earth the royal sage known by the name of Manimat.

That Asura who was the younger brother of Vritra and known as Krodhahantri became noted on earth as king Danda.

That other Asura who was known by the name Krodhavardhana became noted on earth as the monarch Dandadhara.

The eight sons of the Kaleyas that were born on earth all became great kings endued with the prowess of tigers.

The eldest of them all became king Jayatsena in Magadha.

The second of them, in prowess equal to Indra, became noted on earth as Aparajita. The third of them, endued with great energy and power of producing deception, was born on earth as the king of the Nishadas gifted with great prowess.

That other amongst them who was known as the fourth was noted on earth as Srenimat, that best of royal sages.

That great Asura amongst them who was the fifth, became noted on earth as king Mahanjas, the oppressor of enemies.

That great Asura possessing great intelligence who was the sixth of them became noted on earth as Abhiru, that best of royal sages.

The seventh of them became known throughout earth, from the centre to the sea, as king Samudrasena, well-acquainted with the truths of the scriptures.

The eighth of the Kaleyas known as Vrihat became on earth a virtuous king ever engaged in the good of all creatures.

The mighty Danava known by the name of Kukshi became on earth Parvatiya, his brightness as of a golden mountain.

The mighty Asura Krathana gifted with great energy became noted on earth as the monarch Suryaksha.

The great Asura of handsome features known by the name of Surya became on earth the monarch of the Valhikas by name Darada, that foremost of all kings.

From the Asuras called Krodhavasa were born many heroic kings: Madraka, Karnaveshta, Siddhartha, Kitaka, Suvira, Suvahu, Mahavira, Valhika, Kratha, Vichitra, Suratha, Nila, Chiravasa, Bhumipala, Dantavakra, Durjaya, Rukmi, Janamejaya, Ashada, Vayuvega, Bhuritejas, Ekalavya, Sumitra, Vatadhana, Gomukha; the tribe of kings called the Karushakas, and also Khemadhurti; Srutayu, Udvaha, Vrihatsena, Kshema, Ugratirtha, Matimat, and Iswara.

Kalanemi, endued with great strength, became the mighty son of Ugrasena and was known by the name of Kansa.

Devaka was born on earth as the foremost king of the Gandharvas.

Drona, the son of Bharadwaja, not born of any woman, sprung from a portion of the celestial Rishi Vrihaspati.

His son, the heroic Ashwathama, was born on earth of the united portions of Mahadeva, Yama, Kama, and Krodha.

The eight Vasus were born of Ganga by her husband Shantanu.

The youngest of them was Bhishma.

Kripa was born of the tribe of the Rudras.

Sakuni, that crusher of foes, was Dwapara himself.

Satyaki was begotten of the portion of gods called the Maruts.

Drupada was also born of the same tribe of the celestials.

Kritavarman was born of the portion of the same celestials.

Virata was born of the portion of the same gods.

Hansa was born in the Kuru race and became the monarch of the Gandharvas.

Dhritarashtra born of the seed of Krishna Dwaipayana.

Pandu was born of the same father.

Vidura was the son of the Rishi Atri.

Duryodhana was born of a portion of Kali on earth.

The sons of Pulastya (the Rakshasas) were born on earth among men of Duryodhana's brothers.

Dhritarashtra had one son named Yuyutsu, born of a Vaishya wife.

The names of Dhritarashtra's sons according to the order of their birth, beginning from the eldest: Duryodhana, Dushasana, Dussaha, Dussalan, Jalagandha, Sama, Saha, Vindha, Anuvindha, Durdharsha, Subaahu, Dushpradharsha, Durmarshana, Durmukha, Dushkarna, Vikarna, Sala, Sathwan, Sulochan, Chithra, Capachithra, Chithraaksha, Chaaruchithra, Saraasana, Durmada, Durvigaaha, Vivilsu, Vikatinanda, Oornanaabha, Sunaabha, Nanda, Upananda, Chithrabaana, Chithravarma, Suvarma, Durvimocha, Ayobaahu, Mahabaahu, Chithraamaga, Chitrakundala, Bheemavega, Bheemabela, Vaalaki, Belavardhana, Ugrayudha, Sushena, Kundhaadhara, Mahodara, Chithrayudha, Nishamgi, Paasi, Vrindaaraka, Dridavarma, Dridakshatra, Somakeerthi, Anthudara,

Dridasandha, Jarasandha, Sathyasanda, Sadasuvaaka, Ugrasravas, Ugrasena, Senani, Dushparaja, Aparajita, Kundasai, Visalaksha, Duraadhara, Dridahasta, Suhastha, Vatavega, Suvarcha, Adityaketu, Bahawaasi, Nagadata, Ugrasaai, Kavachi, Kradhana, Kundhi, Bheemavikra, Danurdara, Veerabaahu, Alolupa, Abhaya, Dhridhakarmavu, Dhridharathaasraya, Anaadhrushya, Kundhabhedi, Viraavi, Chithrakundala, Pradhama, Amapramaadhi, Deerakharoma, Suveeryavaan, Dheerkhabaahu, Sujaatha, Kaanchanadhwaja, Kundhaasi, Virajasa, and Yuyutsu.

There was also a daughter named Duhsala.

The Kaurava monarch bestowed his daughter Duhsala on Jayadratha.

Yudhishthira was a portion of Dharma.

Bhima was of the deity of wind.

Arjuna was of Indra.

Nakula and Sahadeva were similarly portions of the twin Ashwins.

The mighty Varchas, the son of Soma, became Abhimanyu, the son of Arjuna.